2

THE LEGISLATURE OF THE PROVINCE OF VIRGINIA

ITS INTERNAL DEVELOPMENT

STUDIES IN HISTORY, ECONOMICS AND PUBLIC LAW

EDITED BY THE FACULTY OF POLITICAL SCIENCE
OF COLUMBIA UNIVERSITY

Volume XXVIII]   [Number 2

THE LEGISLATURE OF THE PROVINCE OF VIRGINIA

Its Internal Development

BY

ELMER I. MILLER

AMS Press, Inc.

New York

1967

AMS Press, Inc.
New York, N.Y. 10003
1967

TABLE OF CONTENTS

CHAPTER I

The Beginning of the Legislature under the London Company

PAGE

CHAPTER II

The House of Burgesses—Apportionment, Length of Term, and Qualifications of Members

CHAPTER III

The House of Burgesses—Suffrage, Election, and Judging the Election and Qualifications of Members

CHAPTER IV

The House of Burgesses, Organization and Procedure

CHAPTER V

The House of Burgesses, Organization and Procedure (Continued)

CHAPTER VI

THE GOVERNOR AS A PART OF THE LEGISLATURE

CHAPTER VII

THE COUNCIL AS A PART OF THE LEGISLATURE

CHAPTER VIII

FEATURES OF THE LEGISLATURE AS A WHOLE

INTRODUCTION

ANY attempt at tracing the growth of the legislature in
an American colony meets with many difficulties. One of
these is that commonly the records for the early period are
very incomplete. In a few of the colonies we have no
records of some of the earliest forms of government save
the charters. These are necessarily very general, and therefore show very little of what plans were attempted, and
how far they were successful. A second difficulty is that
the few contemporaneous accounts which have been preserved, written chiefly by those who took part in the
affairs of those times, are, generally, partisan. In fact they
are usually attempts to justify the persons writing them.
Another difficulty is that copies of many of the earlier laws
are no longer extant. The importance of the laws is stated
by Hening in his first volume of the Statutes at Large of
Virginia, when he says, " Indeed, until we come to the
laws of a nation, it is impossible to form a correct idea
of its civil polity, or of the state of society." [1] In addition
to having lost some of these laws, we are handicapped by
the fact that we do not know the reasons the legislators
had for making certain other laws which we do possess,
the arguments used to secure their adoption, and how
fully they were enforced. Occasionally, but only occasionally, tradition throws a sidelight on the actual success or
failure of the laws.

To trace the growth of the legislature of Virginia is not

[1] Hening, *Virginia Statutes at Large*, 1, Preface, iii.

an easy task. There are periods in which one or all the difficulties mentioned above are met. There are also periods when the legislative is indistinguishable from other powers of government, both because these powers were not executed by separate bodies, and because, even when separate bodies did act, their functions overlapped, and they invaded one another's rights.

In the report of the special commissioners sent to Virginia (1676) to inquire into the causes of Bacon's rebellion, the commissioners said that they supposed the Lords of Trade wanted an account of the government as it then was, and not a full history of it from the first settlement. This last they said would be very hard to give " by reason of ye negligence of former times in transmitting anything of that nature to their successors." If there were such difficulties in 1676, how much greater difficulties must now exist, with two and a half centuries more in which records could have been lost and destroyed.

Virginia, like most of the southern colonies, began without any form of local self-government. It had no true legislative body and it had no way in which the people could express their will in government. The colony was established and governed by a commercial company, and not until that company itself took on a political phase and became a center of opposition to the crown, did it think of granting to the colonists any part in the government of Virginia. This grant first came in 1619 with the calling together of the first American legislature at Jamestown. Before 1619 such laws as were made, were enacted by bodies whose chief business was administrative or executive in character. These bodies were the king's council, the London Company, and the governor and council in Virginia. Some of the laws enacted by these bodies reached Virginia in the form of charters; along with these were instructions and ordinances interpretative of these charters.   In such legislation the people could have no part.

From the granting of the first charter to Sir Walter Raleigh, in 1584, to the calling of the assembly of 1619, there were many changes in the form and character of the government of Virginia.   Though it is not desirable to give an extended account of those changes because they did not affect the legislature in any great degree, yet a brief review of them should be given in order to show what the colony was accustomed to at the time the first assembly met.

The grants [1] to Raleigh had made Virginia a private estate of the feudal type.   This gave not only the territorial, but the governmental rights over the province to the proprietor.   No permanent colony was planted under this charter, but it shows to what degree monarchical ideas controlled the minds of those who were interested in colonization.   Under such a system there would have been no place for the governed to take part in governing.

After the lapse of a few years, the idea of the individual estate was replaced by the notion that a commercial company was a far better support for colonization.   It was with this idea that several men in 1605 petitioned for a charter to colonize in Virginia.   The charter was granted to the London and Plymouth Companies April 10, 1606,[2] and under it the Jamestown colony was established.   As Professor Seeley says, this was the beginning of " the creation of a still larger Britain comprehending vast possessions beyond the seas," which was one of the two large movements of the seventeenth century.[3]

A glance at the charter shows it to be very different from

---

[1] *Poore's Charters*, ii, 1379–81.

[2] The old style dates are here commonly used.

[3] Seeley, J. R., *Expansion of England*, 10.

that given to Raleigh. A company under a feudal organization could hardly have been a source of danger to the same degree as an individual with that same power, yet nevertheless the king saw fit to change the type. He did not make a feudal grant, but kept almost all power in his own hands. So much power in the hands of the king was almost as dangerous as it had been in the hands of a private individual. Furthermore with so much power in the hands of the king the company was sure to be weak. So it proved, and the company soon began to ask for more authority. It gradually got more authority until by 1619 it came to have almost entire control. The liberal spirit then dominant in the company led it to share this power with the colonists themselves, through their representatives in the assembly.

Throughout the existence of the company a certain amount of control was exercised by " courts " of the company. These were held in London and soon came to exercise nearly all legislative power save what they saw fit to give to various authorities in the colony. The changes made during the period from 1607 to 1619 were toward freedom of the company, but in no way guaranteed the freedom of the colonists. In fact the governor, appointed by the company in England, recognized no responsibility save to that company. The natural result was that the character of the governor determined the character of the government, though the governor's action was limited by the fear of the company in England.

Under this system either Gates or Delaware introduced a code of laws based on the military law in force in the Netherlands. Later some additions to it were made by Dale and it is known as Dale's Code.[1] It was very severe

---

[1] This code is printed in *Force's Tracts*, iii, no. iii.

in its penalties. Its laws, like all that preceded, were imposed on the people without their consent, and probably in
spite of their opposition. Therefore they form no real
part of the work of a provincial legislature. Although
the governor and council repeatedly spoke of these laws
as operative on the inhabitants generally, it may be but
fair to state that it is doubtful if these laws had application to any except the servants of the company.[1] The
nature of the laws would hardly make them applicable to
the free and independent colonists. Nevertheless the fact
that some of them were in force in the colony for
several years, and that many persons who later were to
have a part in making the laws or at least in electing the
representatives to the assembly, were brought directly or indirectly into contact with them, make it probable they had
some influence on the ideas of those representatives.

The trials of the colony and the trials of the company in
governing it, gradually developed factions in the company
itself. These came to be known as the Sandys-Southampton
and the Sir Thomas Smith (later Warwick) factions.
These factions were to some degree bound up with the
politics of England. They were parts of political parties.
They were therefore subject to the same conditions as political parties everywhere; they were changeable in policy;
they were unstable in their possession of power. The
colonists were then not certain that any form of government they might have at any particular time would be permanent. So long as permanence depended upon parties
and factions whose dividing lines were determined by interests other than those of the colonists, there was not much
hope of a permanent and definite policy. It was nevertheless one of these recurring changes that brought with it that

---

[1] Doyle, *Eng. Col. in Am.*, I, 140.

first factor of stability, the assembly. With an assembly of the people's representatives, a certain permanence was given to both form and policy of government. It was to the Sandys faction that this innovation was due. The accession of that party marked the period of liberal ideas in the company and through the influence of those ideas we have the beginning of the period of self-government in the colony.

CHAPTER I

THE BEGINNING OF THE LEGISLATURE UNDER THE LONDON COMPANY

ALTHOUGH Gabriel Archer is said to have proposed a
" parliament " for Virginia as early as 1608,[1] none was
called before July 30, 1619. Before that date the freemen
of Virginia had taken no part in their own government,
save that performed by the few appointed to local offices
and by members of the colonial council. This was very
little, as the colonists themselves had no voice in the selection of these officials.[2] Indeed, they were often persons
who could not have been chosen by a vote of the people.
Now, a most important change was about to take place.
The instructions of the company ordered the governor to
send out his summons for the election and return of burgesses and to recall the absent members of the council.
The assembly was to meet at Jamestown and was to consist of the governor, the councilors, and two burgesses to be
freely elected by the inhabitants of each plantation, hundred, or ward. The exact basis of representation is uncertain, but it seems probable that any settlement in which
several persons dwelt was allowed to choose members.

[1] Osgood, I, 49; Arber's ed. of *Smith's Map of Virginia*, part ii,
chap. iii, p. 104 says, " Wee not having any use of Parliaments, plaies,
petitions, admirals, recorders, interpreters, chronologers, courts of plea,
nor justices of the peace, sent Maister Wingfield and Captaine Archer
with him, for England, to seeke some place of better imploiment."

[2] *Va. Hist. Collec. New Series*, vii, 76-7, 120-1, 126, 127.

There were twenty-two burgesses chosen, but those from Martin's Hundred were refused their seats for reasons to be given later.

According to Brown[1] the settlements of Virginia were grouped into four large corporations or boroughs. These were composed of smaller boroughs each of which elected two burgesses. The large corporations were the City of Henricus with one borough; Charles City with five boroughs, (Martin's Brandon was excluded in the assembly, leaving but four represented); James City with four boroughs; Kiccowtan with one borough. Brown supposes that the election was by ballot;[2] but, if so, this method was not adhered to, for we find no ballot used in Virginia after 1680, and probably none was before that date. Brown seems to think this arrangement of boroughs and corporations was part of a design to have uniformity of government throughout Virginia as had been ordered by the company.[3]

The names of the members of this assembly,[4] present at Jamestown on the day appointed for the opening of the session, Friday, July 30 (O. S.) 1619, are given in Secretary Pory's report. They met in the church as that was the most convenient place. The governor, Sir George Yeardley, took his accustomed seat in " The Quire " with the council on both sides. John Pory, the secretary of the colony, being appointed speaker, did not now sit with the council as usual, but before the governor with John Twine, Clerk of the assembly, at his side. Thomas Pierse, the sergeant, stood at the bar awaiting the commands of the as-

---

[1] Brown, Alex., *First Republic*, 313-14.   [2] *Ibid.*, 313-14.

[3] *Ibid.*, *English Politics in Early Virginia History*, 28.

[4] W. W. Henry, *Virginia Magazine of History and Biography*, ii, 58-60, says that the members were men of consequence.

sembly. It is important to note that it is probable the speaker was not elected by the burgesses. He was not even one of their number. Yet as a member of the council he was entitled to a seat in the assembly and was thus a member of the body over which he presided. Whether the appointment was made by the governor, by the council, or by the whole assembly is uncertain; but probably it was made by the governor. Doubtless Pory was selected because as secretary of the colony he had an intimate knowledge of the affairs of the colony, and because he was supposed once to have been a member of the English House of Commons.[1] Following the custom of that house the members sat with their hats on.[2]

The burgesses took their places in the choir while Mr. Buck, the minister, opened the session with prayer. When this was ended, the burgesses retired to the body of the church and as each member was called in order by name he took the oath of supremacy and then entered the assembly. When the name of Captain Warde was called the speaker took exception because Warde had no title nor commission for his land. It was the property either of the company, or of Captain Martin, and in either case he was not entitled to represent it. He was ordered to absent himself until the assembly could decide his case. The same day the assembly decided that since Warde had been at great cost and sacrifice to establish his plantation, and had done much for the colony, and that since the commission authorizing the assembly provided for two burgesses from each plantation without restraint or exception, he and his lieutenant should be admitted if he would promise to secure a proper title to his land before the next assembly met. This promise he made and was admitted by an unanimous vote.

[1] See note 6, p. viii, *Colonial Records of Virginia.*   [2] Cooke, 115.

The governor asked that the credentials of Martin's burgesses be examined.   Martin's patent exempted him from obedience to the laws and authority of the colony except in matters of defense.   This was dangerous to the colony and for this reason, Martin's burgesses were ordered to withdraw until he should appear before the assembly in person and agree to surrender that part of his patent.   If he should not surrender it the burgesses were to be excluded entirely as spies, having offered to help make laws they and their constituents were not obliged to obey.   Moreover, Martin's colonists had dealt unfairly with the Indians and caused trouble between them and the whites.   So the assembly ordered a warrant to be issued summoning Martin to appear.   He did so on Monday, August 2, and being asked to surrender the disputed part of his patent, he refused.   His burgesses were not allowed to re-enter the assembly.   The assembly requested the company in England to make Martin's patent consistent with the charter to the colony.   From these two cases we see that from the beginning the Virginia assembly exercised the right to decide the qualifications of members, and to expel members who had been sworn and admitted, if occasion for such action should arise.   The chief qualification decided upon seems to have been subjection to the laws of Virginia.   The case of Martin shows that mere allegiance to the company, or even to England, was insufficient if separated from allegiance to the colony itself.

After the speaker had issued the warrant for Martin's appearance, he made a brief address giving the object of the meeting of the assembly.   He then read the commission for establishing the council of state and the general assembly, and the great charter or commission of privileges, orders, and laws sent from England with Yeardley.[1]

---

[1] The substance of this commission is found in the *Brief Declaration*, 81.

For convenience these privileges, orders and laws were arranged in four books and referred to committees in order that they might see whether they were in perfect harmony with the state of the colony. If not, as this charter was to bind them and their heirs forever,[1] the committees were to prepare petitions to the company to change the orders and laws so as to make them suitable to the colony. The committees, composed entirely of burgesses, having been appointed, the assembly had finished its first half day's work, and adjourned for dinner.

In the afternoon the speaker stated the four objects of the assembly, namely: to consider, first, the great charter of orders, laws, and privileges; second, which of the instructions given to the present and former governors should be enacted into laws; third, what laws might be proposed by the members; fourth, what petitions were fit to be sent home to England. The governor proposed that he and those not then engaged on the other committees should examine the instructions which had been sent to governors.[2] The other committees, after three hours of deliberation, reported, and the assembly adjourned for the day. The committee in its reports on the last two books of privileges and orders found no fault with them; the ratification of these was then put and carried unanimously and with applause. The assembly then ordered the speaker to return thanks to the company for the many privileges granted. With the intention of enacting some of them into laws, the assembly next discussed certain instructions which had been sent to the governors, but after considering some other matters it referred the instructions to the committees previously appointed, and adjourned for the day.

Because of the extreme heat and the sickness of several

---

[1] *Col. Rec.*, 14; Cooke, 116.   [2] Brown, *First Republic*, 317 *et. seq.*

members, the governor resolved to make Wednesday, August 4, the last day of the session. This fact seems to indicate that the governor had the power to prorogue the assembly at pleasure. During this last day the bills which had been considered previously were read a third time and passed. The bills of private members now reached a final reading and passage. The speaker was instructed to engross the laws and to send a copy to each plantation and one to England. The assembly recognized its work as imperfect and sent the following message to the company:

The Assembly doth most humbly crave pardon that in so shorte a space they could bring their matter to no more perfection, being for the present enforced to send home titles rather then laws, Propositions rather then resolutions, Attempts then Achievements, hoping their courtesy will accepte our poore endeavor, and their wisdome will be ready to supporte the weakness of this little flocke.

Governor Yeardley then prorogued the assembly to March 1, following.

The foregoing account gives all that is known of the organization and procedure of the first assembly of Virginia. It had in it many elements of the modern law-making body, though some of its methods, common at that time, have now passed out of use.

The real legislative work of the assembly began on Saturday, July 31, when the petitions prepared by the committees were presented. They asked that former grants of lands be confirmed and new grants be made to the early settlers, that shares of lands be given to all male children born in Virginia, that men be sent to occupy the company lands and to till the lands of the ministers, that rents be made payable in commodities instead of money, that a sub-treasurer to reside in the colony be appointed, that men be sent to build a college, etc. These articles do not have any of the military character of Dale's code. Instead of dealing with the personal control of unruly individuals they relate to legal and economic questions. This feature is also characteristic of the laws passed by this same assembly. It shows that these freemen, representing other freemen, had uppermost in their minds the questions that affected their immediate welfare and safety. The laws refer to the relations the whites were to have to the Ind'ans, to the punishment of idlers, renegades, gamblers, and drunkards, to the payment of church dues, to the planting of corn, mulberry trees, flax, hemp, and vines, to the regulation of trade and the acts of servants, to the regulation of the duties of ministers, to the religious duty of the colonists, and to the conduct of servants. The assembly also acted as a court and tried two cases.

The assembly levied a tax of one pound of tobacco on every male inhabitant above sixteen years of age to pay for the services of its officers, speaker, clerk, sergeant, and provost marshal of James City. This tax was to be received by the speaker, "who not only first formed the same assembly and to their great ease and expedition reduced all matters to be treated of into a ready method, but also his indisposition notwithstanding, wrote or dictated all orders and other expedients and is yet to write several books for all the General Incorporat'ons and plantations both of the great charter and of all the lawes," and the speaker was to distribute the tobacco among the officers according to rank. The speaker was also to report to the company in England. The assembly asked for power to annul the orders of the company as had been promised.

August 4, the governor prorogued the assembly to March 7, following, and in the meantime he dissolved it. This assembly was pre-eminently one of action. They debated little and decided promptly. If we consider that, counting both the day of meeting and the day of adjournment, they were together only six days, one of which was Sunday when they did no business, this first American legislature, in comparison with those of the present day, certainly made a most excellent record.[1]

The acts passed by the first assembly were sent home for the inspection and approval of the company. In the records of the company there are several references to these acts. Sir Edwin Sandys had thought them " in their greatest part to be very well and judiciously carried and performed," and moved that a committee be appointed to draw them into proper heads and forms. On May 11, 1620, the committee apparently asked for instructions, as they said they did not know just what was expected of them; they then asked that others be added to the committee.[2] On May 15, the committee asked for six week's extension of time because the task was so difficult.[3] Whether the task was dropped because of its difficulty, or for other reasons, is not known, but the records of the company give no further information as to the fate of the work of the first American legislature.

Though the assembly of 1619 was prorogued to March 1, 1620, and later dissolved, some authorities say it met in May, 1620;[4] the absence of any account or notice of such

---

[1] Sainsbury, i, 22, gives an account of the assembly of 1619; *Virginia Historical Collection, New Series,* vii, 56, 58, 60; also Bancroft, as before given.

[2] *Manuscript Records,* i, 348.   [3] *Manuscript Records,* i, 357.

[4] Hening, *op. cit.,* i, 119, refers to Beverley as authority but expresses doubts as to any assembly having been held at that date. Beverley calls that the first assembly, though it could not have been the first. Brown says it was customary to take a census just before a meeting of the general assembly, and that such a census was taken in March, 1620. He, therefore, thinks Beverly may have referred to a second assembly,

meeting in the company records makes it somewhat doubtful whether a session was then held.

In 1621, Sir Francis Wyatt, an able man and good governor, was chosen to succeed Yeardley, who wished to retire.[1]   On July 24, 1621, the treasurer and company passed an ordinance providing for the two councils in Virginia;[2] one to be called the " Council of State " and to be chosen by the company, was an advisory council to the governor and was to reside near him in Virginia; the other was to consist of the council of state and two burgesses out of every town or plantation.   The burgesses were to be chosen by the inhabitants of each plantation.   This council was to be called the general assembly.   It was to

have free power to treat, consult and conclude, as well of all emergent occasions concerning the public weal of the said colony and every part thereof, as also to make, ordain and enact such general laws and orders, for the behoof of the said colony, and the good government thereof, as shall from time to time appear necessary or requisite.[3]

The general assembly and council of state were required to follow the laws and practices of the English government so far as that was possible, as was required of the company by its charter.   No law or ordinance of the assembly was to be valid and of force until ratified in a general quarter court

though no record of it exists.   This seems too little evidence to support such a view, for since the company instructed Governor Wyatt, July 24, 1621, to take such a census, and did not connect it with a session of the assembly, census-taking does not seem to be inseparably connected with assemblies.

[1] *Va. Hist. Col.*, vii, 105.

[2] Similar provisions of government were made Nov. 28, 1618 and possibly earlier ; Brown, *First Republic*, 292, 309, 329, 455; see also Chalmer's *History of Revolt*, i, 16.

[3] Hening, *op. cit.*, i, 111–112.

of the company. After the government should be thoroughly settled it was the intention of the company to make no act of the company's court binding on the colony until ratified by the general assembly.[1] This right of double ratification had been promised in 1618, and in August, 1619, the assembly had asked that it be given as soon as possible.[2]

From the commission[3] issued to Wyatt at the time when the ordinance was passed, we find that a majority vote of the assembly was required to pass any measure. The governor had a negative voice or veto.[4] By instructions[5] bearing the same date the governor was ordered to suppress drunkenness, gaming, and excess in dress. Laws for this purpose had been enacted by the first assembly, but as the acts of the session were probably never ratified by the company in England, the governor was to enforce the instructions instead of the law.

Under these instructions Governor Wyatt called an assembly in November or December, 1621.[6] The records of the session are not preserved, but the records of the company show an assembly to have been held at that time. The session seems to have been devoted to carrying out the instructions of the company for the encouragement of the production of staple articles other than tobacco. The adoption of means to encourage the culture of the mulberry tree and the grape vine, and the production of silk and wine took most of their attention. Also some of the wants of the

---

[1] Holmes, *Annals of America*, i, 214-5; Hening, i, 112-3.

[2] Brown, *First Republic*, 321, 456.   [3] Hening, i, 113-4.

[4] In the council as an executive body the governor had a casting vote, but not a veto. This may have applied at a later time in legislation. See instructions referred to in next note.

[5] Hening, i, 114-18.

[6] Stith, and other earlier historians make no mention of this session.

colony were enumerated.   The session was not of any great political importance.[1]

In March, 1623-4 another session of the assembly was held, probably at the same place as before, James City.[2] The first seven articles of their acts are largely concerned with the establishment of churches and the enforcement of religious observances. They show the close connection between civil and religious affairs which then existed and which continued to survive until the revolution of 1776.

One of the most important acts was the eighth, which forbade the governor to " lay any taxes or ymposities upon the colony their lands or commodities other way than by the authority of the General Assembly, to be leveyed and ymployed as the said Assembly shall appoint."   Thus early, do we find the people's representatives demanding control of taxes and appropriations.

In addition to taxation, another form of service to the government, that of personal service, was legislated upon. The governor was forbidden to draw off men from their private occupations to his own service, and in case the public service demanded the help of the inhabitants before the general assembly met, the levy could be made only by the governor and the whole body of the council.   Even then there were limitations, for all planters in Virginia at the time of the last coming of Sir Thomas Gates (1611), and their posterity, were to be exempt from personal service in the wars, and such planters, (but not their families) were to be exempt from all personal dues to the government except those for the church.   This seems to have been an attempt at legislative control of the militia, and to some extent of taxes.

Provision was made that no burgess could " be arrested

---

[1] Hening, i, 119; Brown, *First Republic*, 458, 462.

[2] Hening, 121-9; Chalmers, *op. cit.*, i, 20-21.

during the time of the assembly, a week before and a week after," on penalty of forfeiture of the debt by the creditor and such other penalty as the court might decide. This seems to have been a protection from individuals rather than from the government, the danger against which such a provision is most frequently aimed.

Other acts of this assembly provided for inferior courts at Charles City and Elizabeth City, for settlement of boundary disputes, for levying taxes, for regulating the planting, keeping and sale of corn, for preventing trade with the Indians and for arranging an attack on them in July. It was further declared that persons of quality when delinquent in their duties, " being not fitt to undergoe corporal punishment " should be imprisoned and fined instead. Whatever rumors of changes in the government there might be, obedience to the then existing government was commanded. Mr. John Pountis was sent as a commissioner to the king and his council, thus beginning that system of colonial commissioners and agents which was to become so important in the 18th century. These acts are signed by the governor, seven councilors and twenty-four burgesses. The laws did not reach England in time to be ratified by the company, but most of them were re-enacted by later assemblies.[1]

In the meantime persons in England had made attacks on the company and on the Virginia colony. Two such attacks were published in pamphlet form, and were the " Petition " by Alderman Robert Johnson, former deputy treasurer, and the " Unmasking of Virginia " by Nathaniel Butler.[2] This hostility had caused the company and colonial officials to be very angry and the matter was referred to the assembly of 1623-4. The assembly made separate replies to the two

---

[1] Brown, *First Republic*, 577 *et seq.*   [2] *Ibid.*, 577 *et seq.*

writings and sent them to the king.[1]   In these replies the administration of Sir Thomas Smith was severely criticised and the existing administration praised.

A few days after these replies were completed the privy council's commission was issued to Captain John Harvey, John Pory, Abraham Peirsey, and Samuel Matthews to inquire into the conditions in Virginia, especially as to the desirability of the surrender of the charter and the substitution of direct government by the crown.[2]   This act of the privy council was duly laid before the assembly for its consideration.   The surrender of the charter was demanded. There was no provision in the proposal for any elective legislative body to take the place of the one established under the charter.   This was a direct blow at the existence of a general assembly.   It is quite probable that the English king, James I, would not have seen any need for an assembly.

The assembly saw the necessity of defending itself, but instead of giving a reply to the commissioners, the burgesses decided to deal directly with the king and privy council.   They asked that the governors sent over be given no absolute authority, but be restrained by the council. " But above all we humbly intreat your Lordships that we may retain the Libertie of our General Assemblie, than which nothing can more conduce to our satisfaction or the publique utilitie." [3]   Although the letter to the privy council ignored the commissioners, Samuel Matthews, one of the commissioners, and a burgess, signed it.

After waiting a week for a reply from the assembly, the commissioners addressed a note to the governor, and to the general assembly reminding it of the delay, and submitting a form of acquiescence to the king's will, to be signed by the members.   The general assembly (including

---

[1] Brown, *First Republic*, 570.   [2] *Ibid.*, 571–584.   [3] *Ibid.*, 573.

the governor and council), immediately replied that it had thanked the king for his care over the colony and had returned an answer to the privy council. It added that when consent to the surrender of the charter was required, it would be time to answer further.[1] It expressed the belief that the king's acts were influenced by " much m'sinformation." It then asked to know what further authority the commissioners had. The commissioners explained to some extent, but declined to state their full powers, only saying they would not attempt to wrong any man. That no ill feeling yet existed is seen by the fact that the assembly provided that the several plantat'ons should transport the commissioners from place to place so that they might see the real conditions of the colony. Although the assembly sent its letters direct to the king and privy council, Pory, one of the commissioners, secured copies from the acting secretary, Edward Sharpless. For the offense of giving the copies, Sharpless was pilloried and lost a piece of one ear, though his sentence had been to have his ears nailed to the pillory and then to have them cut off.[2] Thus closed the work of the last Virginia assembly under the authority of the company.

From the time Smith was superseded by Sandys, and a colonial legislature freely elected by the inhabitants was called, Virgin'a began to be a free community in a real sense of the word. True, the acts of the legislature to be valid must be ratified by the company; but the company was in sympathy with liberal government. It desired that the Virginians have a chance to govern themselves. If there could have been any certainty that the company would continue in the hands of such liberal men as Sandys and Southampton it would have been a misfortune for the colony to come under direct control of the crown. But such con-

---

[1] Brown, *First Republic*, 573–4.   [2] *Ibid.*, 583–4; Cooke, 153.

tinuance being very uncertain, it seems probable that in the end it was better the change should come and come early. Doyle[1] says:

The ambitious, enterprising, domineering temper of the Englishman would not suffer him to remain the mere servant of a trading company . . . . As it was, the colony, happily for its future, passed under the control of the crown while it was yet plastic, undeveloped and insignificant. Neither its immediate resources nor any promise of political greatness invited attack till the day had passed when such an attack could be dangerous. During the interval the neglected community was silently maturing its resources, till the Virginia planter, with all his pride of birth and oligarchical temper, was fitted to play his appointed part in the great struggle for national freedom.

In the fall of the company the assembly had no part, hence it is unnecessary to say more than that by the annulling of the charter, July 24, 1624, the hopes for the continuance of the legislature were turned from the acts and promises of the company to the uncertain and apparently unfavorable desires of the king. That there was ground for anxiety will be seen in the later events. The king's frequent interference with the legislature to a considerable extent nullified its powers for the time being. But we shall see that the good seed of self-government sown by the company in the grant of a legislature was not destroyed by such interferences from the king, and after each effort of his to limit its power the assembly soon regained its old position and continued to initiate laws for the freedom of the colony. The place of the assembly, the gradual development of the organ of legislation, and the expansion of the power and influence of the legislature under the royal government from 1624 to 1776 will be the main themes of the succeeding chapters.

[1] Doyle, *English Colonies in America*, i, 183.

CHAPTER II

THE HOUSE OF BURGESSES—APPORTIONMENT, LENGTH
OF TERM, AND QUALIFICATIONS OF MEMBERS

IN any discussion of the Virginia legislature the house
of burgesses must have a leading place. It was the elective
branch, the branch closest to the people and most intimately
in touch with their interests. It was through their representatives in this house that the people took part in the government. It was to this house that they sent their complaints and their demands for redress of grievances. Because
it was so important, the organization and development of the
house of burgesses must be a part of any study of the legislature of colonial Virginia. To give an account of the manner
of choosing members and of the organization and procedure
is the chief purpose of the next four chapters. However,
after the fall of the company (1624) it seems that there were
no sessions of the legislature for a few years. The government was conducted by the governor and council under instructions from England. Therefore before going to the
main discussion it is desirable that the attitude of the English government toward a house of burgesses during this
period be briefly stated, for it will help to explain the relations of crown and burgesses in the years following.

When James had disposed of the company he appointed
a special commission to plan a new form of government
for Virginia, and in the meantime to govern and otherwise
have complete control over the colony.[1] No mention of a

[1] Story, *Commentary on the Constitution of the U. S.*, i, 24.

legislature is made in connection with this commission. What would have been the real government of Virginia we cannot know, for James did not live long enough to work out his plans. However, we can draw the inference that, since James' ideas were not very liberal, it would not have given the legislature an important place. He might, as at the beginning in 1606, have kept all power in his own hands. According to Chalmers [1] two views were then held concerning the status of Virginia; one that it was conquered territory which the king might govern by prerogative alone; the other that it was a dominion of the crown and as such the parliament justly could claim supervision and power of legislation. James held the first of these views and thought the territory should descend to his heirs as a private estate.[2] Of course a legislature was not consistent with this view. Another reason for believing the place of the assembly would have been unimportant is that Sir Thomas Smith, who had allied himself with the interests of the king, was made one of the commissioners. It is not at all probable that he would have favored the continuance of an institution which had criticised his government as severely as had the last assembly under the company.[3] That the assembly feared Smith's influence, is shown by their petition to the king to continue the government as it had been and to keep them out of the hands of Sir Thomas Smith.[4] James' commissioners [5] were to govern the colony until the

---

[1] Chalmers, Geo., *Hist. of Revolt of Am. Colonies*, i, 29.

[2] Chalmers, *Political Annals*, 68.

[3] *Va. Mag. of Hist. and Biog.*, vii, 38–9.   [4] *Ibid.*, 45–6, 129.

[5] The command or commission of these men to plan a new government is given in Rymer's *Foedera*, xvii, 609–13. Extracts from it are found in the *Va. Mag. of Hist.*, vii, 39–43, and in Sainsbury, *Eng. Cal. of St. Pap.* The commission to Yeardley, dated March 4, 1625, a few weeks before the death of James, said nothing of an assembly. See Rymer's *Foedera*, xviii, 311.

new plan was formulated and put into operation. The commission declared that the results in Virginia under the company would have been better if a less popular government had been adopted, and if the control had been in fewer hands. In 1625, shortly after the appointment of the commission, both the king and Sir Thomas Smith died, and whatever plans had been in contemplation came to naught.

Though Charles I was said to hold the same ideas of government as his father, James I, and though he was autocratic in temper, the sequel shows that he was more inclined to give the colony fair treatment than was James. Nevertheless he declared his intention to bring the government of the colony into harmony with that elsewhere in the monarchy, and in May, 1625, he issued a new constitution.[1] By this constitution two councils were to be appointed, one resident in England, the other in Virginia. All colonial officers were directly dependent on the crown. Even with a legislature this dependence of the officers would have prevented that legislative control over them which the assembly later exercised and finally fought to maintain. And, indeed, there is no evidence to show that Charles at first meant to revive the assembly.[2] There is some reason to believe that he was prejudiced against it. An instance to show this is his attitude in the case of Sharpless,[3] the clerk of the assembly, who had been punished for giving out to the privy council's commissioners copies of the assembly's address to the king. This event had occurred before the accession of Charles, but he took this action of the assembly as an offense to himself as well as to his father. Although Charles manifested no particular friendliness toward an assembly, he was not unfriendly to the colony, for Sir Francis Wyatt, a friend of liberal government, was continued as

[1] Doyle, i, 189.   [2] Chalmers, *Pol. Annals*, 112–13.   [3] See page 32.

governor under the new concessions until 1626, and was then succeeded by George Yeardley, a man of like views. That fact must have gone far to reconcile the colonists to the royal control.

It was probably in 1629 that Captain Harvey in " Propositions Touching Virginia " asked the king to grant a new charter under the great seal " and therein to authorize ye Lords to consider what is fitt to be done for ye ratefying of ye privileges formerly granted, and holding of a general assembly, to be called by ye Governor upon necessary occasions, therein to propound laws and orders for the good government of ye people;" and because it is reasonable that the king's subjects should be governed only by laws approved by the king, the acts should be " propositions only," until ratified by the king under the great seal or by the privy council.[1]   The answer to this request was favorable.[2]

The wording of Harvey's petition would suggest the inference that up to 1629 Charles had made no provision for an assembly in Virginia.   If this is a correct inference, and if Harvey's suggestions to the king were made in 1629, one session of the assembly would seem to have been held without the king's sanction, for a proclamation of the governor and council of April 30, 1628, concerning the planting of tobacco and corn, speaks of the " general assembly " as assenting " upon full debate." [3]   At that time the " old style "

---

[1] Printed in *Va. Mag. of Hist. and Biog.*, vii, 369–71.

[2] " . . . but the governor may be authorized shortly after his first coming into Virginia to call a grant assembly, and there to set down an establishment of the Government, and ordaine lawes and order for the good thereof, and those to send hither to receive allowance, and such as shall be soe allowed to be returned thither under the greate seale and put in execucon, the same to be temporary & changeable at his mat'es pleasure signified under the like greate seale." Printed in *Va. Magazine of Hist. and Biog.*, vii, 371.

[3] He ning, *op. cit.*, i, 130.

date was in use and the year began with March 25, instead of January 1, which makes some confusion when dates in January, February and March, old style, are in discussion, for unless we know whether old or new style date is used we may mistake the year. But April was not one of the months the dates of which are doubtful, so April 30, 1628 must have meant 1628.

Again, a reply of the assembly to a letter from the king is dated March 26, 1628.[1]   It was signed by Francis West as governor, five councilors, and thirty-one burgesses. West was succeeded by Dr. John Pott, March 15, 1628.[2] Although the reply signed by West is dated after his term had expired, it is evident that the letter was prepared by an assembly held during his term as governor, and therefore that it must have been in 1627-8. From this it seems quite clear that a session was held in 1628 before the answer to Harvey's suggestion was given, and probably without authority from the king.[3]

There are no records of acts of the assembly of 1628 other than those given above. Since they are so very few and yet there is evidence that an assembly was held, it follows that the absence of records or of authority for calling an assembly fails to prove that none existed. Other unrecorded assemblies may have been held even before 1628.[4]

[1] Henning, *op. cit.*, i, 134.

[2] Stanard, *Colonial Register;* Hening, *op. cit.*, i, 4, says March 5th.

[3] Tyler, *England in America*, says it was called by direction of the king.

[4] Story, *op. cit.*, i, 24, says: " During the greater part of his (Charles I's) reign Virginia knew no other law than the will of the sovereign, or his delegated agent; and statutes were passed and taxes imposed without the slightest effort to convene a colonial assembly." He goes on to say that it was not until open resistance and demands for redress of grievances were made by the colonists that the king yielded. Then he sent out Sir William Berkeley as governor with authority to issue writs

Howison says that such sessions were regularly held.[1]   The king's commissioners, probably in 1631, recommended that the planters in general assembly have a part in making laws.[2]   The legislature of 1642 gave the prevalence of assemblies under the government of Charles as a reason for opposing the revival of the company.[3]   It seems fair to conclude, then, that there could have been no very long period in Charles' reign without an assembly.   The assemblies gradually began to meet regularly, and naturally came to exercise a larger and larger part in the government of Virginia.

Thus far, as was indicated earlier, an attempt has been made to show the place which the legislature had as a whole in the government of Virginia during the last months of James' and the early years of Charles' reign.   Let us now proceed to a study of the main topic of the chapter, the house of burgesses as a part of the legislature.

As was the case in the assemblies under the company, the membership of the legislature, under royal control, included the governor, councilors, and burgesses, and for a long

for the election of delegates to the assembly.   This is certainly wrong, for Berkeley was not sent out till 1642, and Hening, *Statutes at Large*, i, gives the proceedings of the general assembly for the years 1629, 1630, 1632 (two sessions), 1633, 1640 and 1642.   This certainly disproves Story's statement, as no one would care to perpetrate a fraud of such character as to create these records.   Mr. Stanard in *Va. Mag. of Hist.*, x, 263, shows by Governor Harvey's letters and other sources that the evidence of annual assemblies from 1629 to 1640 is tolerably conclusive.

[1] It is true we have no record of general assembly proceedings from 1624 to 1629; "but we have reason to believe that during that time it had regular sessions, and we find the provincial council often relying upon and enforcing its enactments by their own executive power." Howison, 259.   Howison does not say upon what authority he bases his statement.

[2] *Va. Mag. of Hist.*, vii, 38.   [3] Hening, *op. cit.*, i, 231.

time they all sat and voted together as one house. In fact it was not until about 1680 that the assembly permanently separated into two houses, the burgesses forming the lower, and the governor and council composing the upper house. It follows, therefore, that, in some instances what is said in this chapter concerning the burgesses might be said as well of the early colonial assembly as a whole. But while this is true, this chapter refers to the burgesses only. The governor and the councilors as members of the assembly will be discussed in separate chapters.

Since even from the first the body of burgesses was spoken of as "the House of Burgesses," as though it was an organization separate from the rest of the assembly, and because at a later time there were two distinct houses, some method of designation is necessary. Usually they will be referred to as burgesses and council, or lower and upper houses; but it is sometimes desirable to refer to the burgesses as the *house*. The council will never be spoken of as the house, though in its own records of the session of May, 1742, it referred to itself as "the house." This use was exceptional, however, and common usage of the present as well as of that time, will be followed by applying the term "house" to the house of burgesses only.

It has already been stated that the number of burgesses elected to the assembly of 1619 was twenty-two, but that only twenty were allowed to retain their seats. In the assembly of 1623-4 there were twenty-four burgesses. From this time on the number varies with the changes made in the apportionment to each plantation and with the number of plantations or districts. For example, in 1629, twenty-three localities elected forty-six burgesses, and no burgesses appeared for the East Shore; in March, 1630, forty-five members representing twenty-three towns and plantations appeared, and no burgesses for Westover came. Before the

following year these twenty-three plantations were con-
solidated, so that only thirteen districts were represented by
twenty burgesses.[1]   Again, in 1632, twenty-five districts
were represented by forty burgesses.[2]

As early as 1618 the governor and council had received
instructions from the company to divide the colony into
counties,[3] but it is not probable that they did so, for the
records show no acts on the subject before 1634.   In that
year was passed an act dividing the country into eight
shires, each to have a sheriff and lieutenant and to be governed like the shires in England.[4]   This act seems to have
been the first real attempt in the colony itself to establish
counties.[5]   By 1642-3 ten counties had been organized, the
names of which were in several instances different from
those given above.[6]   Some of the names were changed at
this same session.[7]   In this year an act was passed calling
the monthly courts " county courts." [8]   County representation seems to have been adopted for the first time in 1642.
But instead of there being two burgesses from each territorial area as before, a different plan seems now to have
been used; but whether the new basis was one of wealth, of
population, or of size of territory is not known.   The burgesses were apportioned as follows: James City county had
six; Henrico, Charles City, and York counties had three

---

[1] Hening, *op. cit.*, i, 147, 154, 178; Channing, *J. H. U. S.*, ii, 475;
Cooke, 202.

[2] *Ibid.*, i, 178.   [3] Channing, 475.

[4] Hening, i, 224; Channing, 476.   These shires were " James City,
Henrico, Charles City, Elizabeth Citty, Warwick River, Warrosquy-
oake, Charles River and Accawmack."

[5] It is true that several provisions for monthly courts had been made
before this time, but in some cases at least it was provided that they
should be held in certain corporations named, but not in counties.
Hen., i, 125, 133, 163, 168.

[6] Hening, *op. cit.*, i, 239.   [7] *Ibid.*, 238, 249.   [8] *Ibid.*, 273.

each; the remaining six counties, two each. We know the most populous counties had the larger representations and so, as Ingle thinks, the apportionment may have been on a basis of population.[1]   However, this supposition is made doubtful by the words of the assembly of November, 1645, which declare that before that session the number of burgesses had been increased or decreased "without any certain rule for the same." This was stated in the first act, which then provided that in all ensuing assemblies no county, save James City, was to have in excess of four representatives.   James City county was to elect five for the county and one for the city. This rule continued in force during several assemblies, though few of the counties elected four members.[2]   At the session of 1645, there was a member present for the county of Northumberland, though that county does not appear to have been organized and authorized to select burgesses until three years later.[3] A proposition to reduce the number of burgesses to two for each county failed of passage in 1658, but with certain modifications it was carried in 1661.[4]   These modifications were first, that James City, being the metropolis, should have the privilege of electing one burgess for itself; and second, that every county which should lay out one hundred acres

[1] Ingle, *J. H. U. S.*, iii, 181.

[2] Hening, i, 298–299, 322–3, 339–40, etc. Hildreth, i, 339; Foote, 12.

[3] Hening, *op. cit.*, i, 352. This county was first mentioned in Act IX, 1644–5, but not definitely. It was represented in the next assembly, and hence Hening, i, 299, note, thinks it was formed by the governor and the council in the interim. Act I, 1648 (Hen., i, 352–3) does not give that impression, for after speaking of the tract of land it says, " that the said tract of land be hereafter called and knowne by the name of the County of *Northumberland*, and from henceforth they have power of electing Burgesses for the said county . . . . which they are authorized to do by virtue of this act to the next sessions of this assembly."

[4] *Ibid.*, i, 498; ii, 20.

of land and people it with one hundred tithable persons should have the same privilege.[1]   For the session of September, 1663, the list of members shows that three counties, James City, Charles City, and Isle of Wight, had three members each.   James City county was entitled to three by the act of 1661, but whether in the cases of the last two mentioned the three representatives were a violation of the act of March, 1661-2, or were due to these counties having planted one hundred tithables on one hundred acres of land, is not known.[2]   The session of June, 1666, shows but one member for several of the counties; only Isle of Wight has three; the others have two.   During the session of October, 1666, Isle of Wight county proposed to dismiss its extra member, but the assembly refused to permit the dismissal, because no burgess was admitted "without legal and deliberate examination of his return," and the house, having so examined and passed upon his returns, was in honor bound to allow him to hold his seat during that assembly.[3] The presence of but one member from several of the counties seems to have had legislative sanction, for by Act VII, of the October session, 1669, it was provided that, because several inconveniences had arisen from the act giving liberty to the counties to choose one or two burgesses at discretion, therefore it was ordered that each county should thereafter send two burgesses.[4]   The inconveniences were that the requirements of committee service, absence from sickness and other causes, frequently deprived counties having only one member of any representation in the house when important matters were before it.   Hening gives no act permitting one member, unless the law of 1661, reducing representatives to two for each county, be taken to mean not more than two,

---

[1] Hening, *op. cit.*, ii, 20; Statutes of 1661, 50.   [2] *Ibid.*, ii, 196, note.
[3] *Ibid.*, ii, 253.   [4] *Ibid.*, ii, 272-3.

with only one if desired by the county; yet, evidently the assembly of 1669 thought that there was such authority and repealed the act providing for it. In the year 1670 it was enacted that any county which failed to send two burgesses should be fined 10,000 pounds of tobacco.[1] A year later it was again declared that each county should have two burgesses, and according to the letter of Governor Berkeley to the home government, each county had the required number.[2] Throughout the rest of the colonial period the law provided for two burgesses from each county, and one from each of such corporations as had secured charters granting that privilege. At various times Willamsburg, William and Mary College, and Norfolk were given such charters.[3] Jamestown had the privilege as early as 1661, but after the removal of the capital Jamestown became a " rotten borough " in that it came entirely into the control of two families who owned most of the island.[4] In the convention of 1775 the College was not allowed a representative. By May, 1776, the delegates had reached the number of one hundred and thirty. From this it is evident that the number of counties had greatly increased.

Some writers have thought that in addition to county and corporation representation that there was a limited parish representation. Ingle says that for some years parishes as parishes, were allowed to elect burgesses, but later, because of the expense, they could send members only when they had measures to advance. The evidence to support

[1] Hening, *op. cit.*, ii, 282; Hildreth, *op. cit.*, i, 525.

[2] Hening, ii, 512. The letter was written 1671.

[3] Jamestown was given the right to elect a burgess in 1661, Williamsburg in 1742, Norfolk in 1736, and the College in 1705. Beverley, book iv, 6–7, printed in 1705, says the college was then entitled to representation. With the exception of 1762 and 1769, all four boroughs are not mentioned in the list of burgesses at any one time.

[4] Stanard, *Va. Col. Reg.*, 9.

this statement is not absolutely conclusive, but such as it is, is as follows. From the first formation of counties in 1634 it seems that the assembly had the formation of new counties and parishes and the determination of boundaries completely under its control. Since representative districts coincided with these local divisions, the assembly also had control of those districts. In a few instances at least the representative district was designated as the parish. For example, the assembly of 1643 fixed the boundaries of Lynhaven parish and further provided that the people thereof should have free liberty to choose burgesses for that parish.[1] This is the first case of parish representation provided for in the statutes, though there were similar cases afterward. Even in this instance it is not certain that the parish alone, as such, chose burgesses, unless the parish and county were co-extensive. At first many parishes were co-extensive with hundreds and counties, and thus they may have been said to send representatives to the assembly. By act LXII of the session of 1643, the assembly ordered " Burgesses for the several parishes " in the upper Norfolk county to be chosen within the limits of said parishes. That county had three parishes but at several of the following sessions had but two burgesses. Occasionally three burgesses appear, but not regularly. Either the parishes did not use the liberty given them or the act referred to something else, as possibly that the parishes were to be election precincts instead of representative units. This interpretation seems hardly plausible however. Moreover in 1658 the assembly ordered sheriffs to hold elections for parochial burgesses when requested to do so by the vestry.[2] As at that date Isle of Wight county had four burgesses, they were prob-

[1] Hening, *op. cit.*, i, 250.

[2] *Ibid.*, i, 545. John Hammond, burgess for the lower parish of Isle of Wight county, was expelled Nov. 1652, Hen. i, 374.

ably representatives of parishes.[1] These cases seem to bear out Ingle's statement.

The length of term for which members were elected was irregular and uncertain. At first it is probable that they were elected to serve during the session only. At times the assemblies for various reasons, and usually in violation of law, held over from session to session, because the proper officials did not care to order another election. This is notably the case from the restoration to Bacon's rebellion, to be referred to later.

Under the London Company, as has already been seen, the term appeared to be limited, in practice at least, to a single session. The constitution of 1621 directed the assembly to be called "once yearly, and no oftener, but for extraordinary and important occasions."[2] These instructions probably were not obeyed after the fall of the company. After 1624 there are no records of meetings before 1628, and then only the barest reference to a session. The instructions sent by Charles I to Governor Berkeley in 1642, ordered the calling of assemblies "as formerly once a year or oftener."[3] Not before 1647 is there found any record which points to a legislature having existed for more than a year after its election. In that case the evidence is not wholly conclusive.[4] Whatever may have been the fact

---

[1] *Va. Mag. of Hist.*, viii, 393, as reprinted from Edmund Randolph manuscript.

[2] Hening, i, 512.

[3] *Va. Mag. of Hist.*, ii, 281–88.

[4] Briefly stated, the evidence is as follows: the assembly met, November 3, 1647, and when they had considered, but not wholly settled, some questions of "Greate and weightie consequence," it was found inconvenient for the members to stay from home at that time of year, and they adjourned to October 1, 1648. (Hen., i, 341.) The next session did not begin until October 12, 1648. The burgesses must have been elected as early as October, 1647, for they began the first

in that instance, it is certain that not long after a case of such extension did occur. In March, 1655, an assembly met, did business, and adjourned till March 10, 1656. That session was prorogued to the following December. This session was held, having begun December 1, 1656. Here is a clear case of violation of the principle of annual election. The importance of the event rests in the question, was it a conscious effort on the part of the authorities to deprive the people of annual elections? With the example of the English long parliament before them, such an attempt would not be unnatural.

In March, 1659, an act was passed providing that a new assembly should begin March 10 of every second year. Was this law making a longer term a new departure or did it give legal sanction of what had already existed in practice?[1] The case in 1656 makes the latter the more probable assumption. When the assembly elected Berkeley as governor the next year, it declared that the burgesses were to be called together every two years or oftener, though we know that during much of the reign of Charles II elections were not held so often. After Bacon's rebellion Charles II confirmed this law in the instructions issued to the governor, directing him to call the assembly only once in two years instead of annually (except in an emergency), and to limit the session to fourteen days unless he (the governor) found good cause to extend the time.[2]

session November 3. The next session beginning October 12, 1648, the actual existence of this assembly must have continued near to, if not in excess of, a year. It is certain that at the second session the assembly adjourned to meet February 10, 1648–9, clearly several months over the year. (Hen., i, 357.) Hening gives no record of the February session, and it is possible a meeting was not held.

[1] Hening, i, 517; Hildreth, *op. cit.*, i, 366.

[2] Hening, *op. cit.*, ii, 424; *Ancient Virginia Records* (MSS.) Lib. of

Before 1660 few assemblies were continued beyond the legal time, though there was one considerable interval (1624-1628) in which it is possible that no session at all was held. After 1660, almost the whole period until Bacon's rebellion was occupied by different sessions of the same assembly. In 1662 the laws were revised. All those omitted from the revised list were declared repealed. Among those omitted was the one requiring biennial elections of burgesses. Bancroft[1] considers that this act was thus repealed by the assembly, but Howison[2] thinks there is reason to believe that such was not the intention. He says elections were held up to 1666, but that the same assembly with the same members held office from 1666 to 1676.[3]

By 1700 the custom of proroguing assemblies from session to session had become very common. The records show from one to seven sessions held by one assembly without renewal by election. However, Beverley (1705) says that the time of meeting of the assembly had been either once a year or once in every two years; " and seldom two entire years passed without an assembly." [4]   In 1762 the burgesses declared frequent new assemblies more satisfactory to the people, and petitioned the king to allow them one new assembly every three years at least.[5]   During the same

Cong., typewritten copy in Va. Hist. Soc. Lib., 99.   The reference in the instructions to annual sessions was not in accord with the practice of the years immediately preceding. This discrepancy may have been due to the fact that instructions given at an earlier date provided for annual sessions, and in making out new instructions they simply amended the old ones without reference to the then existing practice.

[1] Bancroft, ii, 205.   [2] Howison, 326–7.

[3] Hamilton, *Federalist*, 332, says that under the colonial governments elections were "septennial." This is true of the present English House of Commons, unless sooner dissolved, but certainly was not true in Virginia in the early period.

[4] Beverley, book iv, 8.   [5] Hening, *op. cit.*, vii, 518.

session, however, it was enacted that no assembly should continue longer than seven years,[1] and that the assembly then in existence, unless sooner dissolved by the governor, should legally expire May 26, 1768, five and a half years after the passage of the act. In reality none ever existed seven years.

The qualifications required for membership in the assembly are not usually stated in very direct terms; yet there is much that can be inferred from what is found in the records. Many of the references are negative in form, stating who might not be burgesses instead of who might be such; but it is fair to infer that those who did not have the specified disqualifications were therefore qualified. Foote says that qualifications for office were not established until necessity compelled it to be done.[2] This may be the reason that the qualifications for office were more definitely stated in the eighteenth century than in the seventeenth.

The laws of the seventeenth century show few requirements in regard to residence of members. However, it would have been natural for the people to select members who were residents of the districts that chose them. The references in the laws are not to place but to time of residence. They are in reality denizenation or naturalization acts. While it is certain that aliens who had not gone through some process of becoming citizens could not hold office, it is not certain that all who became denizens were made capable of holding office. It is possible some were merely admitted to suffrage but not qualified to hold office. The acts are not clear on that point. That the assembly made a difference between commissions of denizenation and commissions of naturalization, is clear from the record in

[1] Hening, *op. cit.*, vii, 530.
[2] Foote, *Sketches of Virginia*, 13.

Hening [1] where Dutchmen were made denizens and Englishmen were naturalized.[2]   Yet the presumption is that
" free denizens " and naturalized persons were qualified to
hold office; therefore the time of residence required for
denizenation or naturalization may be a possible qualification for office.

Some of the acts for denizenation and naturalization are
as follows: In 1658 a law provided that aliens and strangers might become free denizens when, after *four* years'
residence, they should have taken an oath of fidelity to the
government.   Several Hollanders were thus made free
denizens.[3]   Later, Nicholas Boate, (probably of English
descent), " when he and his family should have resided in
Virginia *two* years and should continue to reside there "
was to receive all the rights of an Englishman.[4]   Bacon's
assembly (1676) declared that only natives of Virginia,
ministers, or persons having resided in Virginia *three* years
could hold office.[5]   This law was re-enacted the following year.[6]   Other references to naturalization are similar
in import.   These references show that foreigners after a
term of residence, varying at different times, could become
citizens, and after that time they might be eligible to the
office of burgess.

The qualifications became a little more definite in the
eighteenth century.   In 1705 the fifth general revision of
the laws was made.   Of the old laws only those reenacted
were to continue in force.   By the revision act all office
holders must be natives of the colony, have been commissioned by the crown, or have resided in Virginia three

---

[1] Hening, *op. cit.*, i, 499.

[2] *Va. Mag. of Hist.*, viii, 393–4, reprinting Randolph MSS. indicates
that only those of English descent could become naturalized to the extent of holding office.

[3] Hening, *op. cit.*, i, 486, 499.   [4] *Ibid.*, ii, 16.

[5] *Ibid.*, ii, 354.   [6] *Ibid.*, ii, 390.

years.[1]   This rule seems to have held until the adoption of the constitution of 1776.

Residence in the county from which elected was probably not compulsory, for Patrick Henry was chosen from Louisa County in 1765, though he was not then a resident of that county.

The minimum age requirement was that members must be twenty-one years old. This was so stated by the assembly as early as March, 1655,[2] and re-affirmed a year later;[3] again also in 1699, 1705 and 1762.[4] Foote states this to have been the usual requirement.[5]

Contrary to the present system, more stress seems to have been placed on the character of the individual than on the age, for many references to character as a qualification are found. The earlier references are to individual cases, one or two of which will show the attitude of the assembly. In 1652 John Hammond, from the lower parish of Isle of Wight county, was expelled from the house of burgesses because he was " notoriously knowne a scandalous person and a frequent disturber of the peace of the country by libel and other illegal practices." [6] At the same session James Pyland, from the upper parish of the same county, was expelled as " an abettor of Mr. Thomas Woodward in his mutinous and rebellious declaration, and concerning his, the said Mr. Pyland, blasphemous chatechisme." [7]

The assembly of 1655 endorsed the principle involved in these cases by enacting that a burgess " shall be such and no other than such as are persons of knowne integrity and of good conversation."[8] This was reaffirmed in 1658. The

---

[1] Hening, *op. cit.*, iii, 251–2; *Spotswood Papers*, ii, 60.

[2] Hening, *op. cit.*, i, 412.   [3] *Ibid.*, i, 475.

[4] *Ibid.*, iii, 174–5, 243–4; vii, 519.   [5] *Foote*, 13.

[6] Hening, i, 374; Cooke, 202.   [7] Hening, i, 374–5; Cooke, 203.

[8] Hening, i, 412.

same year it was enacted that persons guilty of " the odious sinnes of drunkennesse, blasphemous swearing and cursing, scandalous living in adultery and ffornication " were to be held incapable of being witnesses or of holding any public office; in addition to this those who were proven guilty were subject to a fine.[1] Bribers were disqualified, even if the bribe were only promised but not delivered.[2] By the law of 1705 any one who had been convicted of treason, murder, felony, blasphemy, perjury, forgery, or of any crime, which under the laws of England or other country where he had been convicted, was punishable by loss of life or member, was disqualified to hold office civil, religious, or military, unless previously pardoned. If any such person was discovered in office and convicted he was made to forfeit 500 pounds current money and 20 pounds like money for every month he continued in office after his conviction.[3]

That these laws were enforced is evident from numerous cases in which the burgesses expelled or otherwise punished persons of bad reputation who had been chosen to membership in the house. They were punished, however, only after investigation proved the charges.[4]

The year following Bacon's rebellion those who had been prominently engaged in that uprising were made incapable of holding any office except that of constable or surveyor of highways. If, however, the person had returned to duty and helped to suppress the rebellion, the disability did not

[1] Hening, *op. cit.*, i, 433.

[2] *Ibid.*, iii, 242; vii, 526; ix, 57; *Archæologia Americana, Series 4,* vol. iii, 422.

[3] Hening, iii, 250–1. Also *ibid.*, ii, 390.

[4] These cases will be referred to later in connection with the punishment of members, election contests, and judging the election and qualifications of members. Hence further discussion is unnecessary at this point.

apply.[1] Many of the foregoing disabilities are general for all officers, but as burgesses were considered as officers, the disqualifications applied to them as well.

Bruce[2] says that a considerable number of those who became members of the house of burgesses, and of the council, had been indented servants when they had first come to the colony. But when they had served their time and secured the land grant allowed them, they had immediately become active in affairs and by superior ability had made themselves important factors in the colony. Some of these had been of good family in England and had chosen to indenture themselves as servants and apprentices in order to get a good start in Virginia. In the early years of the colony such apprenticeship was not uncommon.

In the early years of the assembly many of the burgesses were men of small estates, but as the colony became more thickly populated and men of large properties became more numerous, most of the officers, burgesses included, were chosen from the wealthier planters and merchants.[3] It is true that in 1711, Governor Spotsword said the assembly was composed of " men of narrow fortunes and mean understandings." Of the assembly of 1713-14, he said, the burgesses are " persons of the meanest capacities and most indifferent circumstances, and whose chief recommendation to the Post is their declared resolution to raise no taxes upon the People for any occasion whatever." Again in 1723, he noticed a tendency toward " excluding the gentlemen from being burgesses, and choosing only persons of mean figure and character." He said the same mean spirit was

[1] Hening, *op. cit.*, ii, 383-4.

[2] Bruce, *Economic Hist. of Va.*, ii, 44-6; Ballagh, *White Servitude in Va.* (*J. H. U. S.*), 82-3.

[3] Bruce, ii, 378.

shown by the burgesses expelling two members " for having the generosity to serve without pay," on the plea that they were bribers.[1]   It is possible that for a time the less prosperous settlers had control of the legislature; but as the assemblies to which Spotswood referred, had ignored his recommendations, it may be that he was prejudiced against the members and understated their wealth and ability.[2]   At any rate, the general statement that the men of wealth and station held most of the positions, is upheld by Colonel Robert Quary, a man who at various times held office in most of the colonies from New York to South Carolina, who by virtue of his office as surveyor general of the customs, was a member of the council in five colonies at one time,[3] and who was a kind of agent of the home government.   In a letter to the Lords of Trade in June, 1703, he said " Her Majesty's Council, the Assembly, the Justices and Officers of the Government," are chosen out of the large land owners.[4]   These land owners were frequently in debt and for some years it was customary for them to borrow large sums from the colony treasurer.   By 1769 the debts to the treasury were very large, and the influence of the large land holders was so great that Ripley says they were almost able to transfer their debts to the public loan office.[5]

[1] Hildreth, *op. cit.*, ii, 326; Bancroft, *op. cit.*, ii, 20.

[2] Ripley, *op. cit.*, 33–4.

[3] New York, New Jersey, Pennsylvania, Maryland and Virginia.

[4] " But in every river of this province there are men in number from ten to thirty, who by trade and industry have gotten very competent estates.   These gentlemen take care to supply the poorer sort with goods and necessaries, and are sure to keep them always in their debt, and consequently dependent on them.   Out of this number are chosen Her Majesty's Council, the Assembly, the Justices and Officers of the Government." See the letter in the *N. Y. Col. Docs.*, iv, 1051; Hildreth, ii, 234 also refers to it.

[5] Ripley, *op. cit.*, 43.

Although there is so much made of character and property as qualifications, character and property alone were not sufficient; for such persons as negroes, mulattoes, Indians and females, even though freeholders, were debarred.[1]

In a time of state churches and general religious intolerance we should expect a religious qualification for burgesses to be prominent; and so we find it. Beginning with 1619 it was the custom at the opening of each session to administer the oath of supremacy to both burgesses and councilors. Save during the commonwealth period, this was probably never omitted. This oath in reality required the members to recognize the established church of England.[2] In 1643, certainly, and probably as early as 1641, Catholics were prohibited from holding any office. If a Catholic secured office and refused to take the oaths of allegiance and supremacy the assembly could try him and upon conviction dismiss him from the office.[3] The same assembly directed the governor and council to compel all non-conformists to leave the country; so they too must have been ineligible to membership in the house.[4] The assembly of 1659-60 passed a very severe act compelling Quakers to leave the colony. After that, if they returned they were considered felons.[5] Although they were not excluded from the colony at all times, it is not likely that they were at any time admitted to the assembly, as the oaths required would not have been taken by Quakers. Even a friendly attitude toward Quakers aroused suspicion. In

---

[1] Hening, *op. cit.*, iii, 251.

[2] *Ibid.*, i, 139, 149 *et seq.* The members were also required to take the oath of allegiance and a special oath of office. For the oath see Hening, i, 378; ii, 206. Case of dismissal for refusal to take oaths, *Journal of Burgesses*, 1793, 4-5.

[3] Hening, *op. cit.*, i, 268-9.

[4] *Ibid.*, i, 277, 341-2.   [5] *Ibid.*, i, 532-3.

1663 John Porter, a burgess, was accused by John Hill, high sheriff of Lower Norfolk, of being "well affected" toward the Quakers and of attending their meetings; he was charged with being so far an Anabaptist as to disbelieve in baptising children. Porter admitted being well affected toward the Quakers, but said it could not be proved that he had been at their meetings. The oaths of allegiance and supremacy were tendered to him, but he refused to take them, and was dismissed from the house.[1] An act against the Quakers was passed at the same session.[2] Charles II did not sympathize with the feeling against the Quakers and directed Berkeley to be lenient and not to molest them.[3]

In 1699 it was enacted that any person denying the existence of God or of the Trinity, or asserting that there are more gods than one, or denying the Christian religion to be true, or the scriptures to be of divine authority, should be disqualified to hold any office, civil or military. However, the accused person might have the penalty removed by renouncing his opinions within six months.[4] Six years later the law was reaffirmed.[5]

In 1653 ministers were forbidden to sit as burgesses and the act declared, " It is unpresidential (unprecedented) and may produce bad consequences." [6]

As a rule a burgess could not hold any other office during his term as burgess. This was especially true in the later colonial period. A few instances will illustrate the

---

[1] Hening, ii, 198; Cooke, *op. cit.*, 221; Howison, *op. cit.*, 320; Weeks, *Southern Quakers and Slavery*, *J. H. U. S.*, extra vol. xiv, p. 23; *Randolph MSS.*, iii, 282 (Va. Hist. Soc. Lib.).

[2] Hening, *op. cit.*, ii, 180.

[3] Neill, *Virginia Carolorum*, 293.   [4] Hening, iii, 169.

[5] Hening, *op. cit.*, 358–9.

[6] *Ibid.*, i, 378. Ministers are not mentioned again till 1775 when they were excluded from the House of Delegates.

custom in this matter. In 1685 Robert Beverley forfeited his seat as burgess by being chosen clerk of the burgesses.[1] Tobacco inspectors were not only excluded from the house but were not even allowed to take any part in the election of members, or even be present at the polls.[2] Finally, in 1742 and 1748 a tobacco inspector could not become a burgess until two years after vacating the office.[3] Sheriffs or others holding places of profit in the government were not eligible to the place of burgess, and burgesses were exempt from being compelled to serve as sheriffs.[4] By the act of 1762 burgesses were prohibited from holding any other office of profit, and the acts regarding sheriffs and tobacco inspectors were reaffirmed.[5] September, 1744, the burgesses called for new elections to fill the places of persons who had accepted office of surveyor, clerk of court, naval officer and councilor.[6] The duties of treasurer, however, were not held to be inconsistent with those of a burgess, for John Robinson was not only burgess and treasurer for a long time, but in addition from 1738 to 1766 he was burgess, treasurer and speaker. Other offices, the acceptance of which caused a burgess to lose his seat, were those of coroner,[8] collector,[9] clerk of the council,[10] and deputy at-

---

[1] *Journal of Council as Upper House*, 1685, 7.

[2] Hening, iv, 481-2. This was in 1736.   [3] *Ibid.*, v, 153; vi, 185.

[4] *Ibid.*, iv, 292; v, 516; vii, 529; *Jour. of Upper House*, May, 1730, 14 etc. In 1684 a sheriff of Northampton was elected burgess, but was not allowed to take his seat. *Va. Mag. Hist.*, x, 237.

[5] Hening, vii, 529; viii, 95.

[6] *Jour. of Burg.*, Sep., 1744, 3; Feb., 1754, 5; Oct., 1754, 4; April, 1757, 5. Stanard, *Va. Col. Register*, 9-10, says that when a burgess vacated his seat by accepting an office, he was always eligible for re-election except when he became sheriff or coroner.

[7] *Va. Mag. of Hist.*, ix, 355.

[8] *Jour. of Burg.*, Nov., 1753, 30; Oct., 1754, 73; Oct., 1764, 99, etc.

[9] *Ibid.*, May, 1740, 3.   [10] *Ibid.*, July, 1771, 2-3.

torney of the county court.[1]   A councilor while under displacement or suspension could not become a burgess.

The convention of 1775 extended the prohibition of office holding by burgesses so that any person then or thereafter appointed sheriff, mayor, or clerk of any county or corporation, or collector of any taxes, duties, or levies imposed by the convention, or appointed to any military office, thereafter established, except those in the minute-men, was not capable of sitting in the convention, and in case such disqualified persons were chosen new elections should be ordered.   This convention being revolutionary, any one holding office under the crown was held ineligible to membership.

A property qualification does not appear in the records until the beginning of the eighteenth century, but it is very probable that it was a real qualification much earlier.   The report of Quary (1703) stated that the members of both houses were men of large estates.   In 1705 it was enacted that burgesses must be freeholders in the county from which they were chosen.[2]   An act of 1769 was similar except that it said the member must be a voting freeholder.   An act of 1744 required the candidate to have had a freehold for one year at least, just before election.[3]   We find some instances in which persons were excluded because they did not have a sufficiently large freehold.   In one case the sitting member was shown to have rights in 200 acres and therefore was declared entitled to his seat.[4]

The charter of Norfolk, 1736, provided that their burgess should have a freehold or visible estate in the borough to the value of £ 200 sterling if he resided in the borough, or £ 500 sterling, if he resided outside.

[1] *Jour. of Burg.*, July, 1771, 2–3.   [2] Hening, iii, 243–4.
[3] *Jour. of Burg.*, 1744, 12.
[4] *Ibid.*, Oct., 1748, 14; Nov., 1753, 74.

CHAPTER III

The House of Burgesses—Suffrage, Elections, and Election Contests

The qualifications required of voters is important as showing how far the mass of the people had a part in the choice of their representatives. Among the express qualifications for voting, residence did not occupy an important place. The assembly of March, 1658, declared that all freemen in the colony could vote; but a foreigner could not be declared a freeman until he had resided in the colony four years.[1] In 1658 the burgesses resolved that persons holding life estates should be allowed to vote in the county where the land was situated.[2] By act of 1699 the voter was required to be a freeholder in the county or town where he voted, but in neither act was anything said as to his place of residence. Six years later resident freeholders are mentioned as voters. The same year all previous acts relating to the election of burgesses were repealed. The law of 1742

[1] Hening, *op. cit.*, i, 475, 486; see also p. 49–51, as a provision for naturalization must apply to voters as well as to office holders. The time of residence was made two years in 1660. (Hening, ii, 16.) Chalmers, *Polit. Annals*, 315–16, says the first Virginia naturalization act was passed in 1676. Though this is probably true in regard to a general naturalization act, before that date there had been numerous special cases of naturalization and denizenation, both of which processes seem to have given the right of suffrage. See references to Hening above. The naturalization by the colony applied to Virginia only and gave no rights in other colonies or in England. Hening, ii, 290; Chalmers, *Polit. Annals*, 322.

[2] Hening, *op. cit.*, iii, 26.

said that the voters of Williamsburg must reside there twelve months immediately preceding the election. Any one who had obtained from the court of hustings a certificate that he had served five years' apprenticeship in the city, and who was an inhabitant and housekeeper within the city at the time of voting, was entitled to suffrage.[1]

The English Parliament,[2] in 1746, passed a general naturalization law which provided that a voter must have resided in his colony seven years, have taken the oath of allegiance and professed the " Protestant Christian faith " before he was entitled to vote. The act did not require residence in any particular county or locality, but simply in the colony. This act was quite generally ignored in Virginia and probably elsewhere.

As has been said, the location of the freehold and not of the residence of the voter was the important requirement. The committee on elections once (March, 1755-6) tried to reverse this by declaring a vote invalid because the voter had not resided on the land long enough. Its decision was overruled by the house.[3] A similar action was taken in November, 1769.[4] From the last case it might be inferred that a man might vote in every county in which he possessed a large enough freehold to entitle him to a vote. Although this was probably not so,[5] Beverley's remark that freeholders only could vote for burgesses and that " wherever they have a Freehold (if they be not women or under age) they have a vote in the election," [6] might seem to point to multiple voting.

---

[1] Hening, v, 205-6.   [2] Thwaites, *The Colonies*, 62.

[3] *Jour. of Burg.*, March, 1755-6, 32-5.

[4] *Ibid.*, Nov., 1769, 85.   [5] Hening, *op. cit.*, viii, 306.

[6] Beverley, bk. iv, 6-7. See also decision of committee on contests for assembly of Feb., 1745. Jour., 48.

In discussing the residence of voters it has been necessary to refer to property qualification as well. This qualification will now be given further attention.

There was a period during the Commonwealth when all freemen, including freed servants were allowed suffrage, " there being no property or other qualification." [1] The restoration assembly of 1670 reversed this on the ground that when all freemen could vote, many who had little interest participated and often caused tumults and disturbances. It declared that since the laws of England restricted suffrage, Virginia would follow her example, and thereafter only " such as by their estates real or personal, have interest enough to tye them to the endeavor of the public good " should vote in Virginia. This interest was said to belong only to freeholders and house-keepers answerable for public levies.[2] This was a part of the general scheme of the wealthy class to control the government, and in Bacon's assembly (1676) was referred to as one of the causes of the rebellion.[3] Bacon's assembly restored the suffrage to all freemen.[4] At the same time it was declared that the James City burgesses should be chosen by the majority vote of house-keepers, freeholders and freemen listed there at the time of the election, providing they were at the same time liable to pay tax levies there. No others were to vote. However, instructions to Berkeley that same year directed him to see that only freeholders should vote for burgesses

---

[1] Hening, i, 333–4, 403, 475, note; ii, 82, 280, 356; Hildreth, *op. cit.*, i, 509; Ballagh, *J. H. U. S.*, xiii, 351; Foote, 13. In 1665 housekeepers were allowed suffrage, but the following year all freemen were again given suffrage—Hen., i, act xvi, 403, 411–12; Bancroft, *op. cit.*, i, 151.

[2] Hening, *op. cit.*, ii, 280; Hildreth, *op. cit.*, i, 524; Bancroft, *op. cit.*, i, 451.

[3] Ripley, *op. cit.*, 30.

[4] Hening, ii, 356–7; Hildreth, i, 543; Cooke, *op. cit.*, 245.

because that was " the more agreeable to the custom of England." [1]   This instruction overthrew the act of Bacon's assembly.

As time went on the instruction given to Berkeley, that only freeholders should vote, became the fixed policy. A freeholder was defined to be a person having real estate, or having right for life in real estate, whether the right was for a period of his own life or that of another person.[2] At first the amount of real estate required for suffrage was not defined, but it was soon fixed at a hundred acres or other greater estates; but, if settled upon, twenty-five acres with a house and plantation should be sufficient. The vote must be given in the county where the land was unless the tract was in two counties, and then the vote was to be cast in the county where the larger part of it lay. A man must be in possession of his lands for one whole year before the election, unless they came to him by descent, marriage, marriage settlement, or devise. In towns freeholders owning as much as a house and lot might vote, or joint tenants either in or out of towns, might combine and cast as many votes as their property entitled them to give.[3] This law followed the English statutes closely.[4] It was passed in 1736 and was intended to prevent the ceding of small parcels of land or the making of leases on worthless considerations, a practice often resorted to solely to make more voters. Any such transfer of land to make voters was subject to a fine of forty pounds sterling, while a person not a freeholder and yet voting was to be fined five hundred pounds of

[1] Hening, *op. cit.*, ii, 425.

[2] *Spotswood, Letters*, ii, 2, says a freed servant who can purchase half an acre of land has an equal vote with the man of the largest estate. This is probably an exaggeration for most of the period.

[3] Hening, *op. cit.*, iv, 476; viii, 306.

[4] Bishop, *op. cit.*, 83, note 6.

tobacco.[1] Just before the Revolution the time of holding land was reduced to six calendar months, and by the act of 1762 the amount of unsettled land possessed was reduced from one hundred to fifty acres. The size of the house was to be not less than twelve feet square.[2] It will be noticed that the property qualifications considered only the size, not the value of property.[3]

Religion was not expressly made a qualification, but the act of 1643 intended to drive out non-conformists,[4] and that of 1660 against the Quakers,[5] indicates that those sects were not allowed the ordinary rights of other citizens, and when persons were known to belong to those sects it is probable that for a time they were disfranchised. Catholic recusants were also disfranchised. The Quakers were admitted to the franchise after 1699.[6]

In addition to the above conditions of franchise there were several classes expressly disqualified. The act of 1699 said no woman, infant or popish recusant could vote. This was renewed in 1705, but with a provision for a fine of five hundred pounds of tobacco for violation of the act.[7]

Of more significance was the law of 1723 by which free negroes, mulattoes, and Indians were disfranchised in elections for burgesses.[8] Servants were added to this list in

---

[1] Hening, *op. cit.*, iii, 172.   [2] *Ibid.*, vii, 518-9.

[3] The alternation between limited and extended suffrage on a property basis may be seen by reference to Hen., ii, 356-7, 362, 425; i, 403, 411-2.

[4] See p. 55; Hening, i, 277, 341-2.

[5] Hening, i, 532-3; compare Bishop, 60.   [6] Hening, iii, 172.

[7] In November, 1762, the committee on elections decided that a man who was charged with being a Roman Catholic was yet entitled to vote, as it had not been proved that he was a recusant convict. *Jour. of Burg.*, Nov., 1762, 70.

[8] Hening, *op. cit.*, iv, 133; vii, 519; Hildreth, *op. cit.*, i, 235-8; Bishop, *op. cit.*, 51, does not seem to have noticed negro disfranchisement before 1762. Bancroft, *op. cit.*, ii, 256-7, says it was effected in 1721, but no assembly met that year.

1742,[1] and as they were not apt to be freeholders they probably continued to be disfranchised, though they were not mentioned in the acts of 1762 and 1769. Persons convicted in Great Britain or Ireland might not vote during the time for which they were transported.[2] This was all confirmed in 1769.[3] The convention of 1775 said, " free white men " might vote, and it is fair to conclude that others could not.[4] These references would seem to indicate that the disfranchisement of the negro was general in the later period. In the absence of definite statements on the subject for the earlier years, are we to conclude that free negroes were allowed to vote during those earlier years? Howe says all freemen were allowed to vote in 1655.[5] Bancroft says that before 1721 there was no restriction on the right of the free negroes to vote.[6] Chalmers' *Opinions* states that the lawyer, Richard West, to whom the English authorities had referred the Virginia act disfranchising negroes and mulattoes, declared the law of 1723 invalid, saying, "Although I agree that slaves are to be treated in such a manner as the proprietors of them may think it necessary for their security, yet I cannot see why one freeman should be used worse than another merely on account of his complexion." The government allowed the disfranchising act to stand, however.[7] It was enforced in the assembly of March, 1755-6, when the committee on elections declared

---

[1] Hening, v, 205–6.   [2] *Ibid.*, vii, 519.   [3] *Ibid.*, viii, 307.

[4] *Ibid.*, ix. 58. The editor of *William and Mary Quarterly*, viii, 81, says the restrictions on suffrage were not great in Virginia, and that at the time of the revolution there were twice as many voters in Virginia as in Massachusetts and that the apparent power of the aristocracy depended upon compliance with the popular will.

[5] Howe, *op. cit.*, 67. Howe may have made his statements regarding suffrage too general, as he has regarding townships.

[6] Bancroft, ii, 256–7.   [7] *Ibid.*, ii, 256–7; Chalmers, *Opinions*, 439.

ineligible two men who had negro blood in their veins.[1] It would seem then that negroes possessing the regular qualification of voters were granted the franchise until 1723 and then were permanently disfranchised.

By act of 1661-2 voters were privileged from arrest on the day of the election of burgesses, except for " riotts, ffelony or suspicion of ffelony or escape out of prison when under execution." [2]

Compulsory voting appeared early in Virginia. Professor Hart says: " The earliest and latest laws on the subject were passed in Virginia." Eight different acts appear.[3] The assembly of 1646 provided for a fine of one hundred pounds of tobacco for every freeman who failed to appear at elections and vote, unless he was lawfully excused.[4] In 1662 the fine was increased to two hundred pounds of tobacco.[5] No proxy was allowed.[6] Compulsory attendance at elections was far more important then than now, because at that time elections were a kind of deliberative assembly where questions and candidates were openly discussed and decided upon. Plymouth was the only other colony which had compulsory voting throughout its history.[7] Maryland and Delaware were the only others which had compulsory voting at general elections.[8]

The management of elections of burgesses followed closely the forms used in elections to the English House of Commons.[9]

---

[1] *Jour. of Burg.*, 32–35.   [2] Hening, ii, 86; iii, 248.

[3] Hart, *Practical Essays on American Government*, 43. Acts were passed 1646, 1662, 1705, 1763, 1788, etc.

[4] Hening, i, 333–4.

[5] *Ibid.*, ii, 82, also acts of 1705 (Hening, iii, 238), and 1762 kept the 200 pounds fine.

[6] Bishop, *op. cit.*, 139.   [7] *Ibid.*, 190.

[8] *Ibid.*, 192.   [9] *Ibid.*, 98, 155.

The subject of colonial elections has been treated in a monograph by Cortland F. Bishop.[1] But except in one brief paragraph he does not treat elections in Virginia separately from those of the other colonies, and even in that paragraph he does not separate elections of burgesses from general elections; hence it is here necessary to give as full a discussion of Virginia colonial elections as the records will permit.

At first it was customary for the sheriff to go from plantation to plantation to collect the votes. A law of 1639 enacted that the sheriff should not compel any man to go off the plantation where he lived to vote.[2] It is possible that this method was in use only before counties became representative units, and when the plantation was a voting unit or precinct. The law of 1639 was repealed in 1644. Meanwhile (1640) in Upper Norfolk county the burgesses were to be chosen within the limits of the parishes, of which that county had three. It seems in that case that the parish, although not co-extensive with the county, was nevertheless the election precinct.[3] In 1645 the seat of the county court was made the place of holding the election and the polling place was the county court house throughout the rest of the colonial period.

Before 1775 there was no definite time at which the election should be held. But in that year the convention of delegates first declared that it must be held in April; later, in October, but set no particular day.[4] When vacancies occurred or the regular election was prevented at the proper time, special elections might be called.[5]

[1] Bishop, *Colonial Elections, Columbia University Series.*

[2] Hening, *op. cit.*, i, xix–xx, 227; *Robinson MSS.*, 220 (Va. Hist. Soc. Lib.).

[3] Hening, *op. cit.*, i, 250–1, 277.

[4] *Ibid.*, ix, 54; *Arch. Am., Ser.* iv, vol. iii, 420–1.   [5] Hen., ix, 99–100.

When an election had been determined upon, writs were issued by the proper authority and sent to the sheriffs of the various counties. In England writs for parliamentary elections were issued by the Lord Chancellor, Lord Keeper or Lords Commissioners of the Great Seal.[1] In Virginia the issuance of writs of election was first in the hands of the governor and then of the assembly. It was restored to the governor, and in 1660 was given to the secretary.[2] The law of 1705 ordered that the writs were to be signed by the governor or commander-in-chief and the seal of the colony affixed.[3] Writs for special elections were usually issued at the request of the house itself.

In case the proper officer failed to send out the writ, the sheriff was to call the election without it.[4] It was the sheriff's duty to give notice to the people of the time and place of holding the election. This notice must be given at least six days before election day.[5] In the early period house-to-house notice was usually given,[6] but by the act of March, 1661-62 the sheriff was required to send copies of the writs to all ministers and readers, who were to read the notices on two successive Sundays after services under penalty of heavy fine for neglect.[7] By the law of 1705 the governor, after signing and sealing the writs, was to deliver them to the secretary at least forty days before the time appointed for the assembly to meet. Within ten days after the date of the writs, the secretary was to transmit them safely to

[1] Bishop, *op. cit.*, 106.

[2] Hening, *op. cit.*, ii, 22. The laws of 1661-2 (p. 49) provided a heavy fine for the secretary if he failed to send the writ to the sheriff in time to give legal notice to the voters.

[3] Palmer, *Cal. of St. Pap.*, i, introd. xxxv, says that the writs were signed by the governor; Beverley, bk. iv, 6-7.

[4] Hening, i, 517.   [5] *Ibid.*, i, 300.   [6] *Ibid.*, i, 411.

[7] *Ibid.*, ii, 82; iii, 237-8 (1705); Bishop, *op. cit.*, 112.

the sheriffs of the counties, and they in turn, within three days, were to cause copies (with notice of the time and place of election of burgesses endorsed thereon) to be delivered to the minister or readers of every parish. The election was to occur at least twenty days after the sheriff received the writ. The minister was to publish these notices after service every Sunday until election. He then was required to certify to the sheriff that the writ had been duly published according to law. In case of failure to do as here commanded the secretary incurred a fine of forty pounds current money, the sheriff two thousand pounds of tobacco, and a minister or reader one thousand pounds of tobacco. Thus the system which was inaugurated in 1662 with some modifications became permanent. Everybody was supposed to attend church services, and since dissenting voters were not numerous in Virginia it is probable that only a few were not thus directly notified. Save that the fines were increased, this system continued unchanged up to the time of the revolution.[1]

The officers of election provided for in the laws are those already mentioned, viz: the governor and secretary who sent out the writs, the minister who published them, the sheriff who arranged for and presided at the elections in the various counties, and then made returns to the secretary, and later the county clerk who kept a record of the returns. Clerks were mentioned in the last part of the period, though some of the contests would seem to indicate that each candidate furnished his own clerk. Clerks are not mentioned in the records for the earlier part of the period.

The method of casting the vote at first seems to have been by subscription. That is, a paper, possibly headed by

---

[1] Hening, *op. cit.*, vii, 520.

the name of a candidate, was handed about. To this paper
the voters subscribed their names, so that at the end of
the voting the combined lists gave the total of the votes
for each candidate and the names of those voting for
each candidate.[1]   This method did not require the personal attendance of the voters at any one place, was
more public, and gave fewer opportunities for corrup-
tion.   Nevertheless it was made illegal after October,
1646,[2] but seems to have been used for a time after that
date.[3] However, personal attendance at elections gradually
came to prevail. The same reason as that for compulsory voting — that of making the elections deliberative
bodies—induced the legislature to require personal attendance.   Both requirements were made at the same time.

The law of 1699 declared that if the election could not be
determined " upon view by the consent of the freeholders
present," the sheriff or h:s deputy should appoint as many
persons as he should think best to take the poll.[4]   The
persons so appointed were to " sett down the names in writing of each freeholder and for whom he shall poll."   Voters, excepting Quakers who make affirmation only, might be
required to take the oath.[5]   The law of 1705 contained the
additional provision that the clerks and others appointed
by the sheriffs must take an oath.   At that time the vote
was to be taken as follows: the clerk " shall write down
the names of all the candidates, every one in a several
page of the book, or in a particular column; and then the
name of every freeholder coming to give his vote shall

---

[1] Hildreth, *op. cit.*, i, 339; Foote, *Sketches of Va.*, 13.

[2] Hening, i, 333-4.   [3] *Ibid.*, i, 403.

[4] In 1693, however, it seems a poll was required to make the election
valid. See *Jour. of Burg.*, Mar., 1693, 9-10.

[5] Hening, *op. cit.*, iii, 172; iv, 476-7.

be fairly written in the several pages or columns respectively, under the name or names of such persons as he shall vote for." [1]   Every voter could vote for two persons, but he need not vote for both of these at one time. After all votes offered were received, the sheriff was to make declaration three times from the court house steps, and if no more freemen offered to vote, he was to conclude the poll.   The law of 1762 was very similar, but required the voter to cast both his votes at the same time instead of allowing him to vote twice, voting for one candidate each time,[2] and empowered and required the sheriff at the request of candidates or their agents to continue the election to the next day if necessary in order to allow all to vote.[3]

The following excellent description of a Virginia election at the beginning of the nineteenth century (and which Ingle [4] says is similar to those of the earlier periods), is taken from the *Baltimorean* of October 27, 1883:

All voted openly and aloud without the intervention of the sneaking ballot.   The candidates sat on the magistrate's bench above.   The sheriff stood at the clerk's table below ; called every voter to come, and announced how he voted.   The favored candidate invariably bowed to the friend who gave him his vote, and sometimes thanked him in words.   All over the court-

---

[1] Hening, iii, 239; vii, 521.   [2] *Ibid.*, vii, 521.

[3] *Ibid.*, *op. cit.*, vii, 521-22.   The journal of the burgesses for May, 1742 (pp. 54-5), records an election contest in which the sheriff (because of a drunken riot) on promise of indemnity by the candidates, postponed the conclusion of the election to the following day.   The law then did not permit this.   The candidates refused to sign the indemnity bond and so the sheriff re-opened the poll and declared elected the candidates having the highest votes.   These persons were unseated by the burgesses.   It seems probable that the law did not provide a distinct time for opening or closing the polls, and the sheriff was allowed to use his own judgment.   See *Jour. of Burg.*, Nov., 1769, 9-10.

[4] Ingle, Edw., *J. H. U. S.*, iii, 182.

house were men and boys with pens and blank paper who
kept tally, and could at any moment tell the vote which each
candidate had received. . . . . . . The election over and the
result proclaimed by the sheriff from the court-house steps,
forthwith the successful candidates were snatched up, and
hoisted each one on the shoulders of two stalwart fellows
with two more to steady them, and carried thus to the tavern,
. . . . . . where there was a free treat for all at the candidate's charge.[1]

When the polling of the votes closed, the sheriff had to
make a return of the results of the election. At first this
return was made to the secretary's office only, but later
he was required, under oath, to deliver copies of the original poll to the county clerk to be placed on record.
Heavy penalties were provided for any failure to make
such a return or for a false return. In the last half of the
seventeenth century the tendency was to impose a heavy
fine.[2] Later the offending sheriff was called before the burgesses, and if he could explain his failure to make a return,
or could amend his return to the satisfaction of the house,
he was discharged.[3] Otherwise he was subjected to such
punishment as the law or the house might provide. If only

---

[1] Quoted in the *Baltimorean*, Oct. 27, 1883, from an article by W. O.
Gregory, in the " Farmer and Mechanic " of Raleigh, N. C.

[2] In 1659 a fine of 2000 pounds of tobacco was imposed for failure to
make returns. (Hen., i, 532.) In 1670 a false return might incur a
fine of 20,000 pounds to the use of the county and 10,000 to the use of
the aggrieved person, with addition of all costs and damages. (*Ibid.*,
ii, 356–7.) In 1660 the assembly fined Martin Baker, high sheriff of
New Kent, for "undue proceedings" in the election of burgesses.
(*Ibid.*, ii, 33.)

[3] A few instances where explanations were required are given in the
following references: *Jour. of Burg.*, May, 1742, 8; Oct., 1755, 9;
March, 1755, 6, 28; Oct., 1710. *Cal. St. Pap.*, i, 142, etc. Also explanations for failure to make returns: *Jour. of Burg.*, Oct., 1755, 9;
March, 1756, 16–17; March, 1756, 57–60; April, 1757, 12, 44–5; Nov.,
1761, 18, etc.

some small technical point of the law was unfulfilled the clerk of the house corrected the return.[1]

Judging the election and qualifications of members was an important step in the process. It will be remembered that the legislature of 1619 refused to admit two burgesses because it judged them not properly qualified. In November, 1652, the burgesses carried this so far as to expel two members whose characters were considered inconsistent with the high standard expected of burgesses.[2] There are many other instances in which the house asserted its control over elections of its own members.[3] The case of Isle of Wight county which had returned three members contrary to the law then in force, already has been referred to.[4] The decision of the house that " since no burgess is admitted without legal and deliberate examination of his returns, that it cannot consist with the honor of the house to dismiss him from attendance during the continuance of that assembly of which he is a member," sums up the whole power belonging to the assembly, and shows it to have full and exclusive authority to decide on the qualifications and return of members.

The first record of something resembling the modern committee system for examining election returns appears in the orders of the assembly of 1663, when such a committee was appointed to examine the election returns of newly elected members.[5] The committee on privileges and

---

[1] A few references: *Jour. of Burg.*, May, 1742, 8; Oct., 1755.

[2] Hening, i, 374-5; see p. 51.

[3] The assembly of 1659 decided a contested election case in favor of the return made by sheriff. (*Ibid.*, i, 514.) There was also a case where the sheriff was fined for taking too active a part in the election. (*Ibid.*, ii, 33, etc.)

[4] Hening, *op. cit.*, ii, 253; see p. 43.

[5] Hening, ii, 198; *Randolph MSS.*, 281.

elections grew in importance until in the eighteenth century many pages of the journals of the house are filled with the reports of that committee. After the committee was established it would seem that the usual process was to refer to the committee such matters as election contests, charges against members, breaches of privilege, etc. The committee either investigated directly or provided for investigation before justices of the peace, then made its report and recommendations to the house. Occasionally the house settled such questions without referring them to the committee. During the time the case was under consideration in the house, the member whose case was under discussion withdrew.[1]

Most of the occasions for examining into elections were furnished by contests. Contests were made in Virginia much as in England, either by petition or by " scrutiny." [2] This last meant simply an examination of the poll-list. In England tie votes were decided by the House of Commons, but in Virginia the sheriff, if a freeholder, decided by returning either member he pleased.[3]

The method of procedure as laid down by the assembly of September, 1744, was that the petitioner (or his agent) who brought the contest, should give to the sitting member a list of the voters objected to, with the objections to each. The sitting member should then do the same thing for the petitioner. Sometimes this had to be done within three days, sometimes within ten, and sometimes no time was stated.[4] In some cases the evidence seems to have been given directly before the committee. In others, probably those counties at a distance, evidence as to the qualifications of voters was taken before justices and then certi-

---

[1] *Jour. of Burg.*, May, 1742, 37.   [2] Hening, vii, 522.
[3] *Ibid.*, vii, 522.   [4] *Jour. of Burg.*, March, 1756, 10, 12, 13, 18, etc.

fied to the committee. The voter, even though he had taken oath to owning a freehold, was yet subject to examination by both sides as to whether he had a freehold, how long he had possessed it, and whether or not he had paid quit rents for it, etc.[1]   In case the house thought that a contest petition was frivolous and vexatious, the expenses of the sitting member in defending himself were assessed on the petitioner.[2]   The recommendation of the committee was usually accepted by the house, but the fact that occasionally a case was referred back to the committee or the recommendation entirely rejected shows how vigorously these contests were sometimes fought out. Either party could have an attorney and sometimes the clerk of the committee on contests was allowed to serve in that capacity.[3]

Although we do not have a full record of the committee's proceedings and of the evidence that came before it, the journals contain the substance of its reports to the house. A careful perusal of these reports reveals much of the inner workings of the elections for burgesses, as well as something of the character of officials and candidates. For this reason some of the more interesting of the very large number of contests will be related here. Doubtless there were cases where the laws were stretched in order to qualify some one to vote; and it is certain that then, as now, fraud was sometimes practiced and occasionally with success. This was probably the case in the election in Elizabeth City county for the assembly of November, 1762, when evidence was presented to the committee to show that one man who for years had been so demented that he did not recognize his

---

[1] *Jour. of Burg.*, Sept., 1744, 10–11; Feb., 1745, 13; Nov., 1762, 70, etc.

[2] *Ibid.*, Feb., 1745, 16, 51; Mar., 1756, 70, etc.

[3] *Ibid.*, Feb., 1745, 33; Mar., 1756, 6–7.

friends on the street, was on the day of election fully in possession of his senses and competent to vote. The evidence presented to show his competency was that he had asked who was ahead and when told that his candidate was behind he had asked to be carried to the polls to vote, and that on the way his shoe having fallen off he had known enough to stop and have it picked up. The committee decided that the man was in his right mind at that time and therefore a legal voter.[1] From all the evidence presented in the many contests, to be referred to later, it is fair to infer that elections in colonial Virginia were not more ideal than our elections of the present day.

It sometimes seemed that people took advantage of election contests to stir up scandal or to gain some private advantage. In the contest of John Tabb against William Wages of Elizabeth City county, 1755-6, the right of two persons to vote rested on their claim to the same land. One of these had occupied the land for several years; the other held deeds and said the occupant was illegitimate and could, therefore, not get valid title from his reputed father. Only the man who had valid title to the land was the legal voter; hence it followed that whoever the committee should decide had a right to vote, could claim by this decision a presumption of title to the land. As to the legitimacy of the occupant, the committee wisely said, " your Committee did not think proper to enter into the Examination of that Point." Nevertheless it decided that the occupant and not the other man was entitled to vote.[2]

One of the most frequent grounds of contest was that of treating at election or before. The law prohibited treating after the election writ had been issued. Yet the testi-

---

[1] *Jour. of Burg.*, Nov., 1762, 27-31, 36.

[2] *Ibid.*, Mar., 1755-6, 32-7, 58.

mony showed that this law was not strictly enforced. Violation of this act was in a certain sense regarded as bribery, and for that reason will be associated with other bribery cases.

Though laws concerning bribery in elections had long before been enacted in England, in Virginia they first appeared in 1699. Then it was provided that any gift of money, meat, drink, or provisions for votes, would make the election void. Even a promise to give anything to influence a vote, disqualified the promisor to sit as a burgess.[1] By the law of 1762 the time within which treating was prohibited was extended so as to begin with the dissolution of the assembly.[2] After a few years this was modified so as to allow the candidate to entertain in his own house in the ordinary course of hospitality.[3]

These were the legal provisions; but in 1745 the burgesses passed a resolution for their own guidance as follows:

Resolved, That if it shall appear any Person hath procured himself to be elected, or returned a Member of this House, or endeavoured so to be, by Bribery or any other corrupt Practices, this House will proceed with the utmost Severity against such Person.

Resolved, That if it shall appear that any Person hath been tampering with any Witness, in Respect of his Evidence to be given to this House, or any Committee thereof, or directly or indirectly, hath endeavoured to deter or hinder any Person from appearing or giving Evidence, the same is declared to be a high Crime and Misdemeanor, and this House will proceed with the utmost Severity against such Offender.

---

[1] Bishop, *op. cit.*, 197; Hening, *op. cit.*, iii, 173. This was re-enacted in 1705, Hen., iii, 243.

[2] Hening, vii, 526.   [3] *Ibid.*, viii, 313–4.

At the same time they adopted the committee report to prevent treating after the issue of writs for election of burgesses.[1]

The need for the resolutions is shown by a contest that was reported by the committee just a short time after the adoption of these resolutions. It was the case of Francis Epps against Stephen Dewey of Prince George county. The evidence shows, that on the evening before the election nearly eighty voters of that county, some of whom lived more than thirty miles distant, went to the home of Dewey, and, because it was very cold and the ground covered with snow, were entertained over night at Dewey's, where they were supplied with food, shelter and rum; that Mrs. Dewey said she was busy all night giving out rum; that at least one and perhaps several voters were drunk the next morning; that neither Dewey nor any one for him had invited these people to come, or had at any time solicited votes for him; that most of those present voted for him the next day, but had intended to do so even before they went to Dewey's; that one person who voted for Dewey said although he had promised to vote for him, he would not have done so if he had not gone to Dewey's that night; that on election day Dewey's wife employed a neighbor and friend to take some of Dewey's negroes and a hogshead of punch to the court house; that the friend put the punch about a hundred yards from the door, arranged the faucet, tasted it to see if it had enough spirit in it, and then went into the court house; that soon after the voting began, Dewey's negroes, in the absence of the neighbor, invited the freeholders to drink, and said those for Dewey could drink as much as they pleased; that two witnesses testified that William Hall, a son of Dewey's wife,

---

[1] *Jour. of Burg.*, Feb., 1745, 19–20.

intreated several persons to drink; that Dewey had not known of, or ordered these things done, and on election day he had refused to treat before the poll was concluded; that when Dewey's friends had heard of the punch they had gone to the hogshead, pulled out the faucet and stopped it up. Such was the testimony. The committee declared that Dewey had not been at fault and therefore had been duly elected. The house sustained this declaration by a vote of fifty-three to seven. The petitioners were assessed Dewey's costs in defending himself.

This decision was reached on Saturday and on the Monday following Mr. Conway who had made the report of the committee on contests on Saturday was ordered to bring in a bill to prevent giving or selling strong drink on election day before the polls closed. He brought in the bill the next day.[1] It would hardly be expected that an assembly that had failed to see the weak points in its decision of the Dewey case, would be able to provide for a law to remedy the evils there shown; and in fact, neither at that session or at any other of that assembly does any such law appear to have been passed.[2]

Another instance occurred in the election to the assembly of April, 1757. A contest made on the ground that the candidate had treated, was opposed on the plea that the treating was not done by the candidate or by his orders. Nash, the sitting member, admitted that when the bill for liquor was presented to him after the election, he had paid it. Such bills had been paid by all other candidates except the contestant who had refused to pay for any save " a Tickler of Rum and a Bottle of Rum " which he had ordered. The house decided in favor of Nash.[3]

[1] *Jour. of Burg.*, Feb., 1745, 59 ff, 67.

[2] Hening, *op. cit.*, v, 310–407.

[3] *Jour. of Burg.*, April, 1757, 56. A side piece of evidence was to the

In general it may be said that where the evidence was to the effect that the candidate knew of the treating he was commonly held to be disqualified to hold the seat, and if he did not know of it he was not disqualified.[1]

An arrangement between the member and the person contesting to withdraw the contest or to exclude certain evidence was regarded as corrupt and sufficient ground for declaring the seat of the sitting member vacant, and the ordering a new election.[2] An offer to serve without pay, made for the purpose of influencing votes was considered bribery.[3]

Punishment for violating the election laws has already been referred to incidentally in other connections, but a few additional cases will be noticed. In April, 1684, a sheriff was fined two thousand pounds of tobacco for making an improper return.[4] In 1745 some candidates gave a written promise to oppose county or parish division and thereby got many votes. It was held that these men were not duly elected.[5] Any one interfering with the election was subject to punishment either of a reprimand by the house, a fine, or such other penalty as the house determined upon.

Vacancies were filled by special elections managed in the same way as regular elections were. The few cases mentioned in the early record do not indicate definitely who

effect that a merchant had offered to pay costs of a suit against Nash (if the plaintiff could prove that Nash had been at fault in the suit), providing the said plaintiff would vote for Nash. He so voted.

[1] *Jour. of Burg.*, May, 1740, 41–2; May, 1742, 37; March, 1755–6, 23, 32–5; March, 1756, 58; 1772, 101; etc.

[2] *Ibid.*, May, 1742, 38, 41, 57.

[3] *Ibid.*, March, 1755–6, 32–5; Chalmers, *Hist. of Rev.*, ii, 71.

[4] *Virginia Mag. of Hist.*, x, 238.

[5] *Jour. of Burg.*, Feb., 1745, 73.

issued the writs for such elections,[1] but it seems probable that they were issued as in regular elections,[2] from the secretary's office, probably on notice of a vacancy from the house. At a later time the house asked the governor to issue writs to fill vacancies. The act of 1699 provided that the sheriff should appoint a sufficient number of persons to notify the freeholders of the time and place of the election to fill vacancies.[3] This law was re-enacted in 1705,[4] in 1762,[5] and again in 1769.[6] After the overthrow of the royal government, the president of the convention was directed to issue an order to the sheriff or the clerk of the county committee to call an election to fill the vacancy.[7] In some respects this followed the plan in use in England, as when parliament was not in session the speaker made a request to the king's secretary to issue writs calling elections to fill vacancies.[8]

[1] Hening., *op. cit.*, i, 374–5, 493.   [2] *Ibid.*, ii, 105, 203, etc.
[3] *Ibid.*, iii, 174.   [4] *Ibid.*, 241.
[5] *Ibid.*, vii, 525.   [6] *Ibid.*, viii, 312–13.
[7] *Ibid.*, ix, 55. *Am. Arch. Ser.*, iv, vol. iii, 421.
[8] Bishop, *op. cit.*, 110, cites Geo. III, chap. 41.

CHAPTER IV

THE HOUSE OF BURGESSES—ORGANIZATION AND PROCEDURE

OFFICERS were one of the first essentials in the organization of the house. In the records of the seventeenth century the only officers mentioned are speaker, clerk, and sergeant-at-arms. Yet it is probable that a chaplain, doorkeepers, and messengers always present in later times, were also a part of the machinery of the earlier period. The mere absence of any notice of these officers is not conclusive evidence that they were not present, for Hening says nothing even of a speaker from 1619 to 1646 [1] though it is reasonably certain that there was such an officer at every session of the assembly. So there might have been other officers and yet no mention may have been made of them. The office of treasurer [2] was probably one of later development, the money at first being in control of the royal officials. It was realized that control over the treasurer would mean a more certain control over the disbursement of money, and that to elect him was to have power to control him. At first the whole assembly elected the treasurer,[3] but gradually the burgesses secured the privilege of keeping money, as well as money bills, in their

[1] Hening, i, 322.

[2] A royal treasurer was appointed from 1636 to 1693, when the office became elective. *Va. Mag. of Hist.*, ix; Stanard, *Colonial Register*.

[3] Hening., *op. cit.*, iii, 93. The first treasurer elected by the assembly was Col. Edw. Hill, 1691.

own control.   They elected the treasurer usually from their own number, and from 1738 to 1766 the same man held both the offices of speaker and treasurer.[1]

The title of the presiding officer was "speaker," and it was never changed till the convention of 1775, when he was called president.[2]   When the assembly came together for the first time one of its earliest duties was to choose a speaker for the house of burgesses.   Nothing relating to the manner of choosing the speaker appears in the records before 1653.   At that time the governor and council sent a letter to the assembly advising them not to elect Lieutenant Colonel Chile as speaker, because he was interested in a vessel soon to arrive, and the vessel was to be a subject of discussion by the assembly.[3]   After taking the oath, the burgesses sent a committee of four to the governor and council to learn their reasons " wherefore they cannot joyne with us the burgesses in the business of this assembly about the election of Lieut. Coll. Walter Chile for speaker of this assembly."   At last Chile was elected speaker by a " plurality " vote, but on his own request he was allowed to resign so as to give his attention to his private affairs.   William Whitby of Warwick county was then chosen to the place.   From this case it would seem

[1] The house once said that money should be paid out only on its order. (Hartwell, Blair and Chilton, 62.)   In 1758 the governor was instructed by the home government to separate the offices of speaker and treasurer, but the separation did not take place until eight years later.   Then upon the death of the incumbent he was found indebted to the colony to the amount of £100,761.

[2] *Arch. Am. Series*, iv, vol. iii, 421; also Jour. of Convention.

[3] Upon its arrival the ship was declared forfeit, and was sold to Chile for £400, the appraised value.   The sale was made by the assembly, and the bill of sale executed by the governor and the speaker of the assembly.   It is not strange therefore that the governor and council should have had objections to Chile.   Hening, *op. cit.*, i, 382, 385.

that the speaker was chosen by the assembly, and that the governor and council as a part of the assembly had a voice in his election; that is, the choice was a right of the whole assembly and not of the burgesses alone.[1]   Nevertheless the burgesses of 1659 by a unanimous vote chose Edward Hill as speaker and his election was confirmed by the governor,[2] and this last seems to have been the regular method of choosing after that date.   Even at this session the burgesses asked the governor to assist them in preparing an address to the Lord Protector, asking the confirmation of the privileges they then possessed, especially the election of their own officers.[3]   The same man was frequently re-elected speaker by several succeeding assemblies.   John Robinson served as speaker for about twenty-five years,[4] though he was not always re-elected without opposition.[5]

The speaker's duties were those ordinarily belonging to the presiding officer in that age, such as presiding over the deliberations of the house, signing bills after passage by the assembly, and acting as spokesman for the house. Just before the revolution his powers were somewhat extended.   In at least one instance a tie vote was decided by the speaker's vote.[6]   For his services he received a salary which ranged from 6,000 to 10,000 pounds of tobacco annually.[7]

Although the secretary of the colony was not in the strict sense an officer of the assembly, his office had of necessity close relations with the legislature.   The king appointed to this office, but sometimes indirectly through the governor.

---

[1] Hening, *op. cit.*, i, 377–9.
[2] *Ibid.*, 505–6, note.
[3] *Ibid.*, 512.
[4] Tyler, *Patrick Henry*, 56.
[5] *Jour. of Burg.*, May, 1742.
[6] *Ibid.*, Nov., 1769, 144.
[7] Hening, i, 424 (1656); ii, 38 (1660–1).

The clerk of the burgesses was for a time elected by that body. But in 1686 James II wrote to the governor directing him to dismiss Robert Beverley, clerk of the burgesses, because he had dared to discuss the veto power of the governor, and because he had refused to surrender the records of the house of burgesses.[1]   The governor was directed to appoint some one else as clerk and to see that the new clerk did the work. However, the king directed that the assembly should continue to pay the clerk.[2] Francis Page was appointed by the governor.[3]   This seems to have established a precedent and the governor continued to appoint to this office. In 1693 the burgesses tried to recover their "antient usage and custom" of choosing their own officers,[4] but as late as September, 1744, and probably till the revolution, the clerk still held office by commission from the governor.[5]

There is some confusion in the records in the use of the term clerk. In the journal of the upper house the clerk is sometimes called the clerk of the council and sometimes clerk of the general assembly.[6] In most references the house clerk was the clerk of the burgesses and the clerk of the council was the clerk of the assembly. The governor appointed the clerk of the burgesses in the presence of the council in the council chamber.[7]   The clerk of the

---

[1] Hildreth, *op. cit.*, i, 562; *Randolph Papers*, iii, 399, 429–34 (Va. Hist. Soc. Lib.); Hartwell, Blair and Chilton, 28–30, 40. See Hen., iii, 541–71, for documents relating to Beverley.

[2] Hening, iii, 40–1, 550; *Jour. of Coun. as Upper House*, Aug. (1702), 1, 2, 3.

[3] Palmer, *Cal. St. Pap.*, i, introd., xxxvi, xliii, 20.

[4] *Ibid.*, i, xlvi, 33; *Jour. of Burg.*, March, 1693, 8–12.

[5] *Ibid.*, 1744.

[6] *Jour. of Coun. as Upper House*, Nov., 1685, 57, 65.

[7] *Ibid.*, Aug., 1702, 2–3; *Jour. of Burg.*, May, 1740, 1.

general assembly was probably also appointed in a similar way.[1]

Throughout most of the 18th century the house had four doorkeepers and the council one. These were chosen by each house for itself and were paid by appropriations from the general treasury. When a vacancy occurred persons petitioned for the place and the house voted on the candidates. While the house met at Jamestown it was customary to make the parish sexton one of the doorkeepers.[2] In 1772 these officials were furnished a " decent Suit of Clothes " and " a great Coat " by order of the house.

In the middle of the 17th century the sheriff of James City county was acting as sergeant-at-arms.[3] It was the usual custom for the house to elect some one to hold the position of sergeant-at-arms and mace-bearer. Yet about 1752 Thomas Hall presented a commission from the governor and was admitted to that office. Somewhat later in the same session the governor " appointed " Mr. Epps to succeed Mr. Hall, which seems conclusive evidence that for a short period the governor filled the office.[4]

The records do not show whether or not the messenger was a permanent officer, but in 1692-3 when the governor directed the sheriff of James City county to provide an officer to attend the burgesses, the house replied that it had already appointed a messenger of its own.[5] Whether permanent or temporary, this shows that the office was filled by the house itself.

In 1718 the general assembly and general court employed a regular chaplain, to be paid one pound current money for each sermon preached.[6] But it is probable that

[1] Palmer, *Cal. of St. Pap.*, i, 93.   [2] *Ibid.*, 58.
[3] Howe, *op. cit.*, 66.   [4] *Jour. of Burg.*, Feb., 1752, I, 118.
[5] Palmer, *op. cit.*, i, 33; *Jour. of Burg.*, March, 1692-3, 4-5.
[6] Palmer, *op. cit.*, introd., lx.

the house had its own chaplain during most of the 18th century. It was his duty to attend and read prayers each morning about one hour before the regular meeting of the house. For this he was paid a regular salary. The only other officer was a public printer, whose position was created when it became customary to print the session laws and the journals.

Thus we see the burgesses developed a set of officers similar in most respects to those of the present-day legislative body. Since the same body, the English parliament, served as the model for the Virginia colonial assembly and for the modern legislative body, this similarity is to be expected. This account serves to show the similarity and also the order of development of the different officers.

The privilege and immunities of members of the house were never very numerous, consisting of only a few well defined principles. Of these the earliest to be declared was freedom from arrest. It will be recalled that the assembly of 1623, under the company, gave to members this immunity during the session for one week before, and one week after. The privilege was again claimed in 1631-2, and in 1643. On the latter date the time of freedom was extended so that the law should go into effect at the time of the election and continue in force until ten days after the dissolution of the assembly.[1] In March, 1658, the privilege formerly granted to the members of the assembly was extended to their attendants and for the same time as mentioned in 1643.[2] A little later (1661-2) this was so modified that, if the assembly adjourned for more than one month, the privilege should expire ten days after the end of the first session. If the member was arrested during the time between

---

[1] Hening, *op. cit.*, i, 263.   [2] *Ibid.*, i, 444.

sessions and prosecuted to execution, he was to have a suspension of execution ten days before the next session began, and this suspension was to continue till ten days after the close of the session.[1] A law of 1664 provided that no arrest should be made at James City for the period of five days before and five days after the sessions of the general court and of the assembly, unless the person or persons resided in that county.[2] This was plainly the result of an effort to prevent the interference of the local authorities with the general government, and reminds us of the purpose of exclusive congressional control of the District of Columbia.

The privilege of freedom from arrest seems to have been considerably modified in 1705. It was then enacted that members should be " in their persons, servants, and estates, both real and personal, free, exempted, and privileged from all arrest, attachments, executions, and all other process whatsoever (save only for treason, felony or breach of the peace) during his or their attendance upon the General Assembly, by the space of ten days before the beginning, and ten days after the conclusion of every session of the Assembly." [3]   In case an assembly was prorogued more than twenty days process might begin, but it must cease ten days before the beginning of the next session. This was re-enacted in 1762.[4]

Not only were the burgesses privileged from arrest but it would seem they could not waive that privilege without consent of the house. At least, April 13, 1756, the house ordered that Mr. Power and Mr. Clinch have leave to waive their privilege and answer to indictments preferred

---

[1] Hening, *op. cit.*, ii, 107; Laws of 1661–2, 51.

[2] Hening, ii, 213.   [3] *Ibid.*, iii, 244; Beverley, bk. iv, 7.

[4] Hening, vii, 526–7.

against them in the general court then in session. At the same time members of the house were given permission to appear as witnesses in cases where other members were under indictment.[1] A year later it was resolved that privilege from arrest did not apply to cases involving breach of the peace.[2] A court-martial might not proceed against members during a session.[3] Freedom from arrest was extended even to the person employed by the clerk to engross bills and to transcribe business of the assembly.[4]

That it was not the intention to have this privilege used unfairly is seen in a case which occurred in 1764. An execution had been issued by the general court against a burgess's property in slaves, and he was about to use his freedom from arrest to defy the decree of the general court and remove the slaves from the colony, when the house allowed execution to be served.[5]

From the instances here cited it is clear that this privilege was granted partly for the convenience of the individual member (as in case of protection to servants of members), but largely that the public business might not be interrupted for trifling reasons, or by factious or revengeful persons, and that abuse of the privilege was not permitted.

Another privilege of burgesses during the greater part of the colonial period was immunity from compulsory service as sheriff.[6] Appointment to the office of sheriff had been used by the govenor to get rid of burgesses who were obnoxious to himself.[7]

---

[1] *Jour. of Burg.*, Mar., 1756, 40.   [2] *Ibid.*, April, 1757, 14.

[3] *Ibid.*, Sept., 1744, 61.   [4] *Ibid.*, Oct., 1764, 26.

[5] *Ibid.*, Oct., 1764, 71.

[6] For one of several acts see Hening, *op. cit.*, iv, 292.

[7] Hartwell, Blair and Chilton, 28.

Leave of absence was not a privilege belonging to membership, but it was a very common grant by special act of the house itself. Sometimes permission to be absent was granted for but a few days, sometimes for several weeks. Sometimes it was granted because of ill health of the member, sometimes that he might attend to private business matters.[1] The most peculiar privilege was that of getting credit for drinks at the Williamstown ordinaries during sessions. When the assembly was not in session this was not permitted.[2]

During the eighteenth century there seems to have developed the privilege of a member to be protected from slander, and in slander cases the records seem to make little distinction between the privilege of the member and the privilege of the house, for as a rule a slander of even a single member was looked upon as a breach of privilege of the house as well as of that member. Therefore in the following examples no effort will be made to distinguish one sort of privilege from another.

Mr. Fife, a clergyman of Norfolk, preached a sermon which reflected on two burgesses and the committee on privileges was ordered to investigate to ascertain whether there had been a breach of privilege.[3] In 1735, John Doncastle was declared guilty of a breach of the privilege of the house and ordered into custody because he had used abusive language toward a member and had said he would deny that member entertainment if he ever came to the house. Doncastle made excuse that he was irritable because of ill health and asked pardon for the offense. This

---

[1] For some cases of this see *Jour. of Burg.*, Feb., 1772, 14, 63, 113; Sept., 1744, 22; Oct., 1754, 33; March, 1756, 37; Nov., 1769, 124–5. A like case occurred in the council May 8, 1706.

[2] *Jour. of Burg.*, Feb., 1745, 58   [3] *Ibid.*, Sept., 1744, 38.

was considered sufficient submission and, upon paying the costs, Doncastle was discharged.[1]

Another illustration is seen in the case of John Ruffin. Ruffin publicly declared that William Clinch, a burgess, owed him a debt, and having appointed a day for the settlement thereof, instead of paying it, got him into a small room, shut the door, cocked a loaded pistol, and compelled him to sign a discharge of the debt. For the circulation of this report Ruffin was ordered before the bar of the house to answer for the offense of slander. He appeared and declared that he could prove the truth of his statements; he was liberated so that he might get witnesses. A little later Clinch informed the committee that the important witnesses needed for his defense could not then be present and had the case postponed until the next session.[2] It was postponed a second time, but finally the committee decided that Ruffin had proved his charges, and was not guilty of slander or breach of privilege. He was thereupon discharged,[3] and Clinch was expelled.

In another case Leonard Claiborne was charged with slandering both the members from one of the counties. It was charged that Claiborne accused one member of failing to pay his debts, and the other of misconducting himself in the assembly, and because of this misconduct Claiborne had threatened to take him by the nose. Claiborne did not appear to prove the charges, and the committee de-

---

[1] *Jour. of Burg.*, Nov., 1753, 51, 56.

[2] Clinch said one of his witnesses had gone to Georgia, another lived in Carolina, and a third had broken his collar-bone and could not attend. It soon became clear that he did not want the case heard on its merits. This seems to be the same Clinch who had been indicted before the general court; see pages 87–88; *Jour. of Burg.*, Mar., 1756, 16, 22, 25; April, 1757, 11, 30–1.

[3] *Jour. of Burg.*, 1757, 31; *Va. Mag. of Hist.*, viii, 257. Clinch was expelled and forever disqualified to be a burgess.

clared that he had made the charges and that therefore he was guilty of breach of the right and privilege of the house, " by reflecting upon the whole house in general, and some of the members in particular." He was ordered into custody.[1] An assault on or abuse of a member of the family of a burgess, or an assault upon his servant, was regarded as a breach of privilege and the guilty party was brought before the house, reprimanded and made to pay the costs.[2] In May, 1742, during an election contest the sitting member offered to pay all expenses of the contest already incurred if the contest were withdrawn, before any investigation could take place. The house declared this to be an infringement of the liberty of the people, a misdemeanor, and a breach of privilege of the house. For this breach of privilege the sitting member's election was declared void and a new election was ordered.[3] Interfering with an election of burgesses was also declared to be a breach of privilege.[4]

From these and many similar cases it is clear that the house took much care not only to defend its members, but to protect its own good name. To allow an innocent member to be slandered without protest would have invited wholesale abuse and a consequent discrediting of the house itself.

Punishment of burgesses was largely under the control of the house. The preceding discussion shows that the burgesses were protected to a large degree from other individuals and from other branches of government; i. e., from persons and powers outside the house itself. But it

[1] *Jour. of Burg.*, May, 1757, 72–81. Another case is found in *Jour. of Burg.*, Mar., 1756, 49ff ; the case of Doncastle for using abusive language has been given, pp. 89–90.

[2] *Jour. of Burg.*, May, 1740, 33; Feb., 1745, 103; Nov., 1753, 29.

[3] *Ibid.*, May, 1742, 57.

[4] *Ibid.*, March, 1756, 16–7, 57, 60; April, 1757, 12, 44–5.

does not follow that the offenses protected by privilege went entirely unpunished. On the contrary the house was usually quite ready to punish offending members. Of the penalties the house might inflict on its own members, one of the mildest seems to have been censure, coupled with a forced apology.[1] Other penalties were fines, suspension, expulsion and forfeiture of seat.

A fine was a very common penalty for lesser offences. The assembly of 1631-2 ordered that all members of the assembly should attend divine services in the usual place of meeting one hour after sunrise; that failure to do so should involve a fine of one shilling; that absence from the assembly should incur a fine of 2 s. 6 d. After the application of these penalties if any one neglected his duties, he was " to be fined by the whole bodie of the assembly."[2] The series of rules adopted in 1658 made unexcused absence, drunkenness, interruption of a debater, and personalities, punishable by fine.[3] The next year, to prevent a thing which had greatly hindered public business, the assembly enacted that members who failed to attend at the beginning of the session were to be fined 300 pounds of tobacco for every day's absence unless excused by the assembly.[4] This was re-enacted in 1661-2.[5] The same as-

---

[1] Campbell, Charles, *Hist. of Col. Va.*, 228; Cooke, *op. cit.*, 203. In 1654, Wm. Hatcher, a burgess, having falsely slandered Col. Hill (probably speaker), was censured and forced to make acknowledgment of his error before Hill and the assembly. See also *Jour. of Burg.*, Feb., 1745, 33, 46, 57, which states that Samuel Blackwell and Peter Presly, burgesses, were reprimanded by the speaker for their conduct as justices of the peace in their county. Other justices not burgesses were sent for to receive reprimand. Soon after Presly was given leave of absence for his health.

[2] See *Robinson MSS.*, 93; Hening, *op. cit.*, i, 162. Some persons were fined for contempt of the government in 1652, but there is no certainty that any burgess was among the number.

[3] Hen., i, 508.   [4] *Ibid.*, 532.   [5] *Ibid.*, ii, 107; *Session Laws*, 1661, 50–51.

sembly, instead of being dissolved in the usual way resolved to continue itself through another session and adjourned to another time. To prevent a loss of members, before adjournment the assembly enacted that under penalty of 10,000 pounds of tobacco for disobedience, no burgess should accept the office of councilor or sheriff and thus interfere with his duties as a burgess.[1] The assembly of September, 1663, declared that any member who was absent at the third drum on Monday morning should be fined one hogshead of tobacco.[2] The rules of this assembly provided fines for the several offences as follows: absence on roll-call, 20 pounds of tobacco; intoxication, 100 pounds for the first offence, 300 pounds for the second, and 1000 pounds for the third; interrupting a member while speaking, 1000 pounds; the use of personalities between members, 500 pounds; speaking more than once, 20 pounds; " piping it " in the house during the session, 20 pounds. Every Saturday afternoon the house was to dispose of the fines collected for infraction of the rules.[3] Those for the week ending October 27, 1664, amounted to 460 pounds of tobacco, of which the house voted one half " to use of the house," one fourth to the collector, and one fourth to Major Hone on account.[4] This shows that fines were actually levied and collected.

The eighteenth century shows few records of the imposition of fines upon members. Occasionally, however, absenteeism became so troublesome that unexcused absentees were arrested by the officers of the burgesses and brought into the house.[5] If they could not then give an acceptable excuse they were fined. In February, 1754, several members

---

[1] Hening, *op. cit.*, i, 540–1.   [2] *Ibid.*, ii, 205.

[3] *Ibid.*, ii, 206–7.   [4] *Ibid.*, 253.

[5] *Jour. of Burg.*, March, 1756, 56; Palmer, *Cal. of St. Pap.*, i, 58.

were arrested and fined for being absent at the preceding session.[1]

A burgess might forfeit his seat by accepting either in person or by deputy any other office. If after accepting another office he should continue to sit as a member he was fined fifty pounds lawful money. However, the disqualification was not permanent and he might again at a later time be elected and lawfully sit.[2] In 1700 two burgesses who refused to take the oaths forfeited their seats and others were chosen to fill the places.[3] Suspension was occasionally resorted to in order to force a member to submission.[4]

Punishment of members sometimes extended as far as expulsion. In connection with qualifications the cases of John Hammond and James Pyland of Isle of Wight county, have already been referred to.[5] In 1723 two members " for having had the generosity to serve without pay " were expelled. They were considered to be bribers for they had tried to get votes by promising to take no pay.[6]

Expulsion and disqualification were also enforced against men of bad character. Two cases during the session of May, 1742, will illustrate this. One Henry Downs was charged with having helped to steal sheep; it was said that he had once confessed this offense in open court, and had been punished therefor by fifteen lashes on the bare back, by being put into the stocks, and then by being sold into servitude for one year and nine months to pay fees.

---

[1] *Jour. of Burg.*, Feb., 1754, 4, 7.   [2] Hening, iv, 292-3.

[3] Palmer, *op. cit.*, i, 80. Also case of John Porter, 1664.

[4] For one instance see Hening, i, 7.   [5] See page 51.

[6] Hildreth, *op. cit.*, ii, 326; Chalmers, *Hist. of the Revolt*, ii, 71, says this occurred in 1715.

The house declared he was guilty, expelled him and disqualified him to sit in that assembly. The same penalty was applied to William Andrews, whom the committee declared guilty of " many male and scandalous Practices, in the Office of Inspector." That he had been dismissed from the offices of inspector and justice was evidence of his guilt.[1]

In these cases the persons seem to have been disqualified for that assembly only. But in 1764, a Mr. Proser was charged with having antedated deeds with the intent to prejudice the claims of others, and with various other fraudulent acts in that connection, and was expelled and disqualified forever to sit and vote as a burgess. Costs of the prosecution to the amount of 4776 pounds of tobacco were assessed on him.[2] The case of William Clinch has been referred to.[3] In 1773 a burgess charged with passing counterfeit money was arrested and brought to Williamsburg to be tried before the general court.[4] This was a felony and the privilege of freedom from arrest did not apply.[5] But it was a case for the general court and the house did not need to act.

---

[1] *Jour. of Burg.*, May, 1742, 10, 11, 34, 56.

[2] *Ibid.*, Oct., 1764, 101–9.   [3] Pages 87–88, 90.

[4] *Jour. of Burg.*, Mar., 1773, 11, 25–6.   [5] Page 87.

CHAPTER V

The House of Burgesses—Organization and Procedure Continued

Salaries of members and officers at first were not paid in a very regular way. Sometimes the burgess was paid by the county or parish which he represented,[1] sometimes by the colony as a whole;[2] sometimes he was paid in money, sometimes " in kind " (tobacco). Whether county or colony should pay depended upon the decision of each particular assembly. After September, 1756, except in 1760 and possibly in 1762, the salary was regularly paid from the public treasury. In 1642, 1673 and probably in other cases the cost of servants of members was also paid.[3]

By an act of 1660-1, in order to keep candidates from promising to serve for small salaries, the allowance was fixed at 150 pounds of tobacco per day, besides travelling expenses.[4] This act was renewed the following year.[5] But

[1] By counties, probably in 1636 and 1639 (*Robinson MSS.*, 84, 188), 1642, 1656, 1658 and 1671. In 1688 Henrico made appropriation to pay its burgesses' charges for twenty-eight days' service. This seems to indicate county payment for that session though Hening gives no session for that year. (See *Va. Mag. of Hist.*, i, 177.) The assembly of 1730 forced Caroline county to pay its burgesses for the session of 1727. (Hen., iv, 306.) Salaries of the assemblies of May and August, 1755, of 1756, and 1760 were paid by the counties; in 1762 they were to be paid by the county or colony as the case might be according to the " rules and regulations before said." (Hening, vi, 496–8. 557; vii, 57, 366, 527.) They were paid by parishes in 1656 and 1659.

[2] By colony, 1660-1, 1661-2, 1667, 1676, though it is not certain but that the burden was shifted to the counties in 1730, 1736, 1742, Oct., 1755, and Sept., 1756. (See Hening at the dates given.)

[3] Hening, i, 267; ii, 309-10.   [4] *Ibid.*, ii, 23.   [5] *Ibid.*, 106.

the assembly of 1677 declared that the charges of the burgesses were complained of as being too heavy;[1] hence their salaries were reduced to 120 pounds of tobacco and cask per day, allowing two days each way for travelling. Extra allowance was made for horse and boat hire.[2] Mileage was generally allowed, sometimes as a part of salary, sometimes as expenses only. It might be paid at a rate of so much per mile or in a lump sum. In 1775 the rate was ferriage and four pence per mile both ways.[3] But it seems probable that the more common way was to pay the regular salary of burgess for the days on the road as well as those of the actual session, and in addition to pay a part of the travelling expenses, such as boat and horse hire. In 1730 the assembly made a difference in the amount paid, those having come by land receiving ten shillings and those by water nine shillings per day. In the latter case the boat and the services of two boatmen were to be allowed for.[4] Sometimes the assembly fixed the number of days in transit for which the members could be paid.[5]

In 1730 the assembly directed the treasurer to pay the burgesses in money whenever he could do so without depleting the treasury beyond a fixed minimum amount. After 1745 it was the custom to pay in money, though the salary was sometimes stated in terms of tobacco.

The actual amount of the salary at any period cannot

[1] This complaint had been made in Bacon's rebellion. The commission sent over by the king had recommended a reduction and the king had instructed Governor Berkeley accordingly. See *Ancient Va. Records*, typewritten copy in Va. Hist. Soc. Lib., 101, 109.

[2] Hening, *op. cit.*, ii, 398–9. Those members of Bacon's assembly who had acted loyally since the rebellion were also paid. *Ibid.*, ii, 403; iv, 279–80.

[3] *Ibid.*, ix, 56. For other times at other terms see Hening, iv, 523; vii, 527.

[4] *Ibid.*, iv, 279–80.   [5] *Jour. of Burg.*, Nov., 1761, 27.

be given with any certainty, for while the number of pounds of tobacco, or the number of shillings are frequently stated, the real value of both tobacco and shillings was very different at different times, and never the same as their value at present. Unless sick or excused the salary was forfeited for the time a member was absent from the house.[1]

The salary of the speaker during the seventeenth century seems to have been not more than 6,000 pounds of tobacco annually.[2] It also seems that in 1695 pay to the speaker as such, was discontinued and that the burgesses on several occasions after that resolved never again to make such an allowance. But in August, 1702, when the burgesses sent the book of claims up to the council for passage, they had in it an item of 10,000 pounds of tobacco for the speaker. Harrison and Carter, councilors, objected to this item. They said it had been discontinued and ought not to be revived. The council sustained this objection but Jennings, the secretary, asked that his dissent from the vote of the council be entered in the journal. One ground of objection to the claim was that such salary would make the tax burden too heavy on the people at that time.[3] The governor called attention to the fact that pay had been allowed the preceding August, and said the burgesses were the proper judges of the merits and rewards of their own officers. He also showed the evils that would result from a contest over the matter. Nevertheless the council adhered to its position and amended the book of claims. The burgesses refused to accept the amendment. The council started an investigation of precedents but proposed

[1] *Jour. of Council as Upper House*, ii, May, 1722, 42.
[2] Hening, *op. cit.*, i, 424; ii, 38.
[3] *Jour. of Coun. as Upper House*, i, 26–38 (for Aug., 1702).

to refer the question to the Lords Commissioners of Trade and Plantations, in the meantime leaving out of the claims the pay for the speaker. The governor informed the council that in passing the book of claims, " he demanded a privilege to sitt and vote as president of the council." He at last sent a message to the house saying he agreed with it but hoped for some amicable settlement. The speaker then said the conduct of the council was unprecedented and asked that the house declare its privilege, but omit the appropriation for this time. This was done.

In spite of such incidents as this just related, it was generally customary to pay the speaker a salary. However, during the time the office was connected with that of treasurer the pay attached to the two offices was not separate. The speaker-treasurer then got five per cent of the money he handled.[1] In 1766 the offices of speaker and treasurer were separated and the speaker, being supposed to give his time to the public service, was to receive 500 pounds sterling annually. Three years later this was increased to 625 pounds current money.[2]

Other officers of the house seem to have been paid according to the length of the session, or to the amount of work to be done; for several pay rolls were passed differing very much in the amount paid to each. Two cases will illustrate. In February, 1754, the house resolved to pay officers as follows: clerk of burgesses £60; clerk of the general assembly £30; chaplain £15; sergeant-at-arms £20; doorkeepers £5 each.[3] In May, 1765, the house paid the clerk of the burgesses £250; clerk of the assembly £80; chaplain £60; sergeant-at-arms £80; doorkeepers £15 each;

[1] Reply of Gov. Gooch to Lords of Trade, *Va. Mag. of History*, iii, 123.

[2] Hening, *op. cit.*, viii, 210, 394.   [3] *Jour. of Burg.*, Feb., 1754, 12.

clerks of committees from £80 to £30.[1]   These represent extremes.   Pay rolls of other sessions show amounts between these.

In 1745 the sergeant-at-arms was allowed mileage of three pence per mile each way when he was sent to arrest persons; the arrested person must pay it.[2]

In one case at least an officer of the house took a peculiar, but apparently successful method of raising his salary. He was the clerk to the treasurer and he simply paid the addition to himself and put it in the accounts the same as the other part of his salary.   When the house heard of this and was displeased, he sent in a formal petition and the house granted him £25 per year increase in his salary.[3]

Methods of conducting business were in many respects not unlike those with which we are familiar at the present day.   Yet there were essential differences and therefore a full account is necessary to show what was the actual course of procedure.

It will be recalled that in the first assembly, 1619, each burgess was required to take an oath of office.   In 1658 this oath was as follows:

You & every of you shall swear upon ye holy Evangelist & in ye sight of God to deliver yor opinions faithfully, justly & honestly according to yor best understanding & conscience for ye gennerall good & prosperity of this Country & every pticular member thereof.   And do yor utmost endeavor to prosecute that without mingling wth it any pticular Interest of any person or persons whatsoever, So helpe you God & the Contents of this Booke.[4]

---

[1] *Jour. of Burg.*, May, 1765, 151.

[2] *Ibid.*, Feb., 1745, 53.   [3] *Ibid.*, 1745, 115.

[4] *Ancient Virginia Records* (MSS.) in Library of Cong.   This taken from a typewritten copy, pp. 183-4, in Lib. of Va. Hist. Soc.

In addition to this the oaths of allegiance and supremacy, required of all officials under English jurisdiction, was administered. These oaths are first mentioned in the Virginia legislature in 1629 when it was administered to the governor, councilors, and burgesses before any business was transacted.

The opening of a session of a new assembly was a very formal affair. A somewhat detailed account of the assembly of June, 1775, just before the flight of the governor, will show the method of procedure which had been developed and was used during most of this time and in vogue at the close of the colonial period.

When the election returns had been made and the time for meeting had arrived, the members elect assembled in the council chamber where, according to custom, the oath was administered to those whom the clerk of the burgesses had on his list as having been duly returned. The oath was administered by members of the council appointed for that purpose and was to be taken before the members could enter the house of burgesses. They then entered, took their seats, and were told by the clerk of the assembly that the governor commanded their immediate attendance in the council chamber. When they had obeyed the summons, the governor commanded them to return to their house immediately and elect a speaker. After the return, Henry Lee, a burgess, addressed the clerk (" who standing up, pointed to him, and then sat down,") and moved that Payton Randolph be speaker. Randolph was elected and " was taken out of his place by two members, who led him from thence to the chair; and having ascended the uppermost steps Mr. Randolph returned his thanks to the house for placing him again in that elevated station." After his speech was concluded he sat down in the chair and " then the mace (which before lay under the table) was laid upon the table." Henry Lee and the treasurer were then sent to notify the governor and to ask when they should attend on him to present their speaker. By a messenger of his own the governor directed them to attend him immediately in the council chamber. They did so and the governor expressed himself as satisfied with their choice. Thereupon the speaker in the name of and on behalf of the house, laid claim to all the ancient rights and privileges of members, particularly freedom of speech and debate, exemption from arrests and protection for estates; and lastly, for himself, he requested that his errors might not be imputed to the house. The governor promised to defend them in all their just rights and privileges. When the burgesses had returned to their own house, the speaker reported the proceedings just finished and then read a speech the governor had sent to the house. It exhorted the burgesses to work in harmony with England in the settlement of the disputes then existing.

The governor next sent to the house some papers which were delivered at the bar and then read. They were ordered to lie on the table for the perusal of the members. The orders of the day were next taken up and a reply to the governor's speech was ordered to be prepared. A journal of the first continental congress was brought before the house and ordered to lie on the table for the perusal of members until the Monday following when the house should resolve itself into the committee of the whole to consider the said journal. On that same day the proceedings of the convention of March, 1775 were to be considered also.[1]

The closing of sessions was much less formal. It might

---

[1] The foregoing account is based on the record as printed in *Arch. Amer.*, *Ser.* iv, vol. ii, 1185–8; *Jour. of Burg.*, 1772, 2–5.

be by adjournment, either by recommendation of the governor or on the initiative of the house itself. It might be by prorogation, or by dissolution on order of the governor. As these points are to be discussed more fully in a later chapter, further mention of them here is unnecessary.

Every legislative body must have some rules concerning attendance and conduct of members; also it must have rules of order. In the discussion of the punishments of members,[1] reference to some of these rules has already been made. It is unnecessary therefore to state them in detail here. Suffice it to say that fines were imposed for absence, tardy attendance, drunkenness, interruption of a debator, personalities, and speaking more than once on the same question. In 1659 a set of rules was adopted which were, in substance, as follows: No one without first obtaining leave should absent himself when any matter was being debated; each member was to keep good order and give attention to the proceedings; he should address himself with due respect to the speaker and should rise and uncover his head when he debated;[2] private discourse should not take place while public matters were being discussed.

To prevent absences a call of the house was resorted to. When the roll was called excuses could be made for absent members but these excuses were not always accepted; when they were not accepted fines were charged against the member.

The journal of burgesses for November, 1769, gives a long list of standing rules of order adopted by the house. In substance they are as follows:

1. No member shall absent himself without leave or because sick.

2. When the house attends the governor in the council

---

[1] Pages 92–93.　　[2] *Jour. of Burg.*, Nov., 1753, 77; Feb., 1754, 4.

chamber, the several passages thereto shall be cleared of strangers so members may freely pass; no member shall go into or come out of the council chamber before the speaker.

3. No member shall chew tobacco in the house while the speaker is in the chair or while the house is in the committee of the whole house.

4. When any member is about to speak in debate or deliver any matter to the house, he shall rise from his seat without advancing from thence, and shall with due respect, address himself to the speaker, confine himself strictly to the point in debate, avoid all indecent, disrespectful language.

5. No member shall speak more than twice in the same debate without leave.

6. A question once determined stands as the judgment of the house and cannot be drawn into question again during the same session.

7. While the speaker is putting the question no private discourse, no standing up, walking into, out of, or across the house, or reading any printed book shall be allowed.

8. No member shall vote on any question in which he is immediately interested, nor in any case where he was not present at the time the question was put by the speaker or chairman of the committee.

9. Every member present when a question is put on a division must be counted on one side or another.

10. Each day before proceeding to other business, the clerk must state the orders for taking any matter into consideration that day.

11. Unless ordered otherwise by the house bills shall be read and dispatched in the order presented.

12. The clerk shall not allow any papers or records to be taken from the table or from his possession by either a member or any other person.

13. The speaker and 15 members shall be enough to adjourn, 30 to call the house and send for absent members and 50 to proceed to business.

14. When the house is to rise, every member shall keep his seat until the speaker has gone out, then each one is to follow in the order in which he sits.

15. The journal of the house shall be drawn up daily by the clerk and after being approved by the speaker shall be printed without delay.

16. Eleven of the committee of religion, and of privileges and elections, and five of any other committee shall be enough to proceed to business.

17. No committee shall sit during time of divine service.

18. Any member using bribery or other corrupt practices to secure election shall be severely dealt with.

19. Election contest petitions must be presented within 14 days after the member petitioned against has taken his seat.

20. No person entitled to vote for two members, and giving a single vote, can give his second vote during that election.

21. When the house judges an election petition frivolous and vexatious, the house will order satisfaction made to the person petitioned against.

22. Any member may waive his privilege in any matter of a private nature; but having done so he cannot resume it.

23. Original writs to prevent suit being barred by statute of limitations may be sued out, or a bill in equity be filed against a member in spite of privilege, provided the clerk after having made out and signed such, shall not deliver the same during the continuance of privilege.

24. Witnesses summoned before the house or its committees are privileged from arrest coming and going; a

witness can demand pay beforehand from the person by whom he is summoned and he is not obliged to attend until he gets it.

25. Any person interfering with a witness or trying to influence his testimony shall be punished.

26. No person shall be taken into custody of the sergeant-at-arms on any complaint of breach of privilege until the matter of such complaint be examined by the committee of privileges.

27. Fees of the sergeant-at-arms for an arrest shall be 13 shillings, and for every day he keeps the prisoner in custody 13 shillings; for sending a messenger to arrest on warrant of the speaker, 6 pence per mile going and coming and ferriage.

In 1631 was inaugurated the method of re-enacting all the laws the assembly wished to retain and then of repealing all others.[1] It soon became the custom thus to revise the laws at intervals. In this way the statute books were prevented from becoming filled with numerous obsolete laws. Sometimes the revision was made with the idea of stating the laws more clearly.[2]

Sometimes this work was referred to a committee.[3] In 1685 the house proposed a joint committee of the two houses to revise the laws and report to the next assembly. The governor rejected this proposal and proposed in its

---

[1] Hening, *op. cit.*, i, 177; *Robinson MSS.*, 97.

[2] The assembly of 1643 said: " Whereas the many and sundry acts and laws at former Grand Assemblies established in several books and volumes digested have been found very prejudicial to the colony by the Grand Assembly, for reducing the same into a more exact method and order, and for preventing all mistakes or pretenses which may arise from this interpretation or ignorance of the laws in force," therefore all laws not re-enacted are repealed. Hening, i, 239–40.

[3] *Ibid.*, ii, 34.

stead that the laws be considered by the council only and then be reported to the assembly.[1] This plan was rejected by the burgesses. The burgesses renewed their proposal in 1693,[2] but probably with no better success. However, in 1745 the council consented to a joint committee for the same purpose.[3] Sometimes just the laws on some particular subject were referred to a committee for revision.[4] It was customary for the house to instruct its standing committee on courts of justice to report on matters unsettled from previous sessions, what laws have or are about to expire and ought to be renewed, and to act as a kind of permanent revisory committee.[5]

These revised acts, like new acts, had to be submitted to the king for his approval. In 1748 the king refused to ratify a part of the revised acts and they failed; but since all old laws not reënacted were repealed, there was then no law on those subjects. It would therefore seem that the colony might have been better off if it had let the old laws remain instead of revising them.

In the early part of the colonial period there are few references to committees of the house, yet it seems probable that the house made frequent use of them. Even in 1619 several committees were appointed, and as it was a much-used method later, it is probable that the absence of reference to them is due to incompleteness of the records rather than to a lack of committees.

The purposes for which committees were appointed were

---

[1] *Jour. of Coun. as Upper House*, i, 54–5. Hening gives no laws for 1685, though he refers to such a session. (Hen., iii, 40.) The council journal does not indicate the outcome of the difference of opinion on revision, but there probably was no revision again before 1705.

[2] *Jour. of Burg.*, March, 1693, 21.

[3] *Jour. of Coun. as Upper House*, ii, 61.

[4] *Jour. of Burg.*, Sep., 1742, 20.   [5] *Ibid.*, Feb., 1752, 7.

sometimes of sufficient importance to secure a record of the committee. For example in 1660-1 the assembly appointed committees to act during the recess of the assembly, one to prepare an address to the king, another to revise the laws.[1] In 1664 a committee was appointed to examine the public records and arrange for their preservation.[2] Reference has already been made to committees for revision of the laws.[3]

After the two houses definitely separated, about 1680, references to committees are much more frequent. A regular system of standing committees appears; also many special committees and much use of the committee of the whole.

In the committee of the whole the method of procedure was as follows: the speaker left the chair and some member of the house took the position of chairman of the committee of the whole house. The informal discussion then took place and when the committee rose the speaker reoccupied the chair. The member who had acted as chairman of the committee reported the proceedings of the committee, read any resolutions that might have been passed, and then delivered them at the clerk's table. There they were again read. Another reading was required before they could be adopted by the house. Matters were frequently referred to the committee of the whole.

The house made much use of special committees for many different purposes, but especially for preparing bills to be introduced on matters that had been called to the attention of the house, and in the later years for conferences between the two houses.

The greater portion of the committee work was done by

[1] Hening, ii, 31, 34. [2] *Ibid.*, ii, 210-11.
[3] Pages 106-107.

the regular standing committees. The house usually had several of these, each with its own clerk, such as for propositions and grievances, for privileges and elections, for public claims, for courts of justice, for trade, for private causes, and for religion and morals. Later there was a committee of correspondence to deal with the agent of the house in London. The size of these committees varied, but by 1772 they were composed of from fourteen to thirty-two members each.[1] The records are very precise in telling just how reports were made. A member of the committee standing in his place read the report and then handed it to the clerk.[2] Committees had power to send for persons, witnesses, papers, and records.[3] It is probable that the committees were named by the house itself.[4] In the Randolph Papers (III, 76-7, 80-5, etc.) are some committee records. They resemble regular legislative journals and show how the committees did their work.

The daily sittings of the house usually began with prayers by the chaplain at 9 or 10 o'clock, and the business an hour later. In the summer of 1771, the prayers began at 8 and the business at 9 a. m. The object of this was probably to get most of the work done before the heat of the day came on. The sittings lasted several hours.

The process of law-making was about as follows:[5] a bill was introduced, sometimes in answer to a petition, sometimes by direct order of the house, sometimes by the direct request of some member, or by resolution of a com-

---

[1] *Jour. of Burg.*, 1772, 7–9; Oct., 1755, 5–6.

[2] *Jour. of Burg.*, 1772, 12.   [3] *Ibid.*, Sept., 1744, 4.

[4] *Ibid.*, Oct., 1764, 6–8, says: "*Ordered*, That a committee of Privilege and Elections be appointed, of the following persons," and then names the persons.

[5] Taken from the journals of the two houses.

mittee. It was probably not the custom to refer all bills to standing committees as is the present rule in Congress, though this was sometimes done, especially when the measure was of a character suited to one of the standing committees. As a rule, however, most measures were not introduced in the form of bills but rather as petitions, resolutions, etc., and these were referred to interested persons or committees to formulate into bills.

Bills were read twice, then referred to committees for amendments or amended in the house, or engrossed, read again and passed or rejected, (though they might be rejected at any reading by being refused passage to the next reading) then sent to the council by a member or a committee usually composed of members interested in securing the passage of the bill. The council went through a very similar action and, unless it rejected or refused to act on the bill, returned it to the house. If any amendment had been made the house considered the bill again and, if it concurred in the change, passed it. When a bill had been enrolled and approved by the council, it was ready for the signature of the governor, which was given in the presence of both houses in the council chamber. However, if the house refused to concur in the amendment, it sent a message to the council to that effect and sometimes asked for a conference, though this was sometimes left for the council to do. A quotation from the records will show some of the forms of doing business.

The Order of the Day being read, for the second reading of the Bill for appointing an Agent;

The said Bill was read a second Time.

Resolved that the Bill be committed to a committee of the whole house.

Resolved, That this House will, upon Friday next, resolve itself into a Committee of the whole House upon the said Bill.

Occasionally orders of the day were made by fixing a day for second or third reading of some bill; e. g. March 17, 1772, it was ordered that a bill be engrossed and printed and that the third reading be on July 1, next, over three months distant.[1]

In case of a division on a vote, it was the custom for one side to go out of the room; e. g. in September, 1744, a division caused the " noes [to] go forth " and resulted " noes 8, yeas 45." [2] Sometimes a ballot was called for, as in choosing one doorkeeper from several candidates. The clerk passed around " a glass " and each member put in a ballot with the name of the person voted for written thereon. The glass was then brought to the clerk's desk and a committee of six counted the ballots.[3]

The quorum required to do business varied. In 1685 twenty-three burgesses met and said that since they were neither a house nor had a speaker, they could not even adjourn, but must wait for the governor to prorogue them.[4] In October, 1748, the house decided by a vote of 44 to 35, that 41 should be a house to do business.[5] A few years later twenty-five were declared enough,[6] but in 1769 the number was much larger.

It was a common thing to combine two or more totally different subjects in one bill; e. g. one bill was passed to prevent hogs and goats running at large in the streets of

---

[1] *Jour. of Burg.*, 1772, 96. It is probable that they expected to adjourn to meet again about the beginning of the next July. Toward the end of the same session several other matters were postponed in the same way. *Jour. of Coun.*, May, 1744, 24ff.

[2] *Ibid.*, 18; other cases *Jour. of Burg.*, Feb., 1752, 64, 119, etc.

[3] *Ibid.*, 1772, 5.

[4] *Jour. of Coun. as Upper House*, Oct., 1685, 2-3.

[5] *Jour. of Burg.*, Oct., 1748, 4-5.   [6] *Ibid.*, Mar., 1756, 74.

Suffolk, and to give the town permission to hold a fair.[1] The " rider " was sometimes used, both to make an addition to an engrossed bill and so avoid the going over of the whole process of enactment again,[2] and, as at the present time, to carry clauses which could not pass if voted on separately. In the latter class was the bill appropriating £2500 to pay an agent of the assembly in England and attaching it to an appropriation of £20,000 to carry on war. The council protested against the appropriation for the agent,[3] but inasmuch as the agent was finally sent and was paid the house had its way.

Thus did the house carry on its business. Early in the colonial period, then, we find many present-day practices already established. Those of the earlier time were extended and others to suit new conditions were added, the process continuing down to the revolution. Indeed, that the methods of doing business should be similar to present-day practices is to be expected when we remember that the legislature consciously tried to imitate so far as applicable the procedure of the English House of Commons, and that that body had already developed the essentials of present-day practice, (save that growing out of the cabinet system,) when the colonial assemblies were just coming into existence. This was especially true in such things as the opening and closing of parliament, rules of conduct of members, and the process of law-making.

[1] *Jour. of Coun. as Upper House*, Oct., 1748, 27. Spotswood rejected a bill of that kind. *Letters*, ii, 54.

[2] *Jour. of Burg.*, Aug., 1755, 18; Nov., 1762, 88.

[3] *Ibid.*, Aug., 1754, 18.

CHAPTER VI

The Governor as a Part of the Legislature

In all countries where there is a legislature distinct from
the executive, the executive has a greater or lesser part
in legislation. How great that part is depends upon
the country and the age. As a rule, the organization of
the executive has preceded the organization of the legislature, and usually it is true that the executive has granted
the powers which the legislature has possessed.

In the American colonies we find a few exceptions to
this general statement. It was not true in the New
England colonies, for there the executive and the legislature were organized at the same time and got their power
from the same source, the people. Virginia was a partial
exception, for when it was under the control of the Company that body created both executive and legislature.
The chief executive, the governor, was a kind of overseer
of the estate. Yet under the instructions from the company he had a more direct part in legislation than did the
New England governor who was chosen by the people.[1]

When the royal authority was established in Virginia
there was for a time no legislature, and the whole government was in the hands of the governor and other officials
appointed by the king. Some years later the legislature
was re-established, but its powers came as grants from
the executive of the home government through the gov-

[1] Osgood, *American Colonies in the Seventeenth Century*, i, 162–3.

ernor of the colony. Naturally then the governor was an important factor in the organization of the legislature.

The fact is that the executive often by its own needs as well as by the needs of the people, was forced to call upon the people through a legislature to aid in the conducting of government. Professor Osgood has well said: "Like all their other organs of government, the legislatures of the provinces developed as the result of social and political causes operating upon the proprietors and in the provinces themselves. Though not original in the sense in which the executive was, events soon showed them to be instruments of government which were indispensable to proprietors as well as provincials, and about their development center events of the greatest interest in the history of the provinces. Their study reveals the operation of forces which were to transform the fief and thus to open the way for the growth of modern democratic institutions. The rise of assemblies in the English-American colonies is an event of great significance in the history of the world." [1] While Professor Osgood states this as applying to the proprietary province, it applies equally well to the royal province, for it was the needs of the situation that everywhere induced the executive to authorize a legislature and give it an important part in the government.

The development of legislatures was no less important in the royal than in the proprietary provinces, and one of the most interesting as well as important features was the struggle between the legislature and the executive as represented by the governor to get or to keep a controlling place in the government. Among English-speaking peoples in modern times the general tendency has been to lessen executive influence in legislation and strictly to de-

---

[1] Osgood, *op. cit.*, ii, 74-5.

fine the power that is left to the executive. Virginia during colonial times was engaged in the process of limiting and defining executive power. When the revolution came she was so far advanced in this that the first governor of Virginia under a state constitution was almost without power. He was a mere tool in the hands of the legislature. It will be the purpose of this chapter then briefly to indicate (1) the part which the governor of colonial Virginia took in the legislature, what he did and how; (2) how this part was modified, limited and defined from time to time.

In the period during which a unicameral legislature existed the burgesses, council and governor all met as one legislative body. Although in some respects the governor was the most conspicuous member of the assembly, he was not, as in Massachusetts, the presiding officer. From the beginning the assembly had a speaker. As we have seen, in the assembly of 1619 the speaker was the colony secretary; hence he was probably a member of the council.[1] Whether this is true or not, it is very certain that in the many assemblies that followed the speaker was always a burgess. Since the governor did not preside, and had no place of special importance, it may seem fair to conclude therefore that the governor as a member of the assembly was in about the same position as other members, save that being governor he had a veto on measures finally passed and consequently had more personal influence. The real part which the governor had depended much on his instructions, but even more upon the personality of the man.

So far as the records of the early colonial period show, the part of the governor as a legislator stands out much less prominently than his judicial and administrative functions. Such information as they give deals largely

---

[1] See page 20.

with the external and formal things, such as calling, proroguing, and dissolving the assembly, vetoing acts, etc. From the amount of attention given him in the records then it would seem fair to assume that as an individual the governor was less prominent in legislation than in other lines.

In spite of this conclusion from the records, however, during the unicameral period the governors were quite generally the dominant force in the government, even the legislature being quite docile at most times. This was noticeably the case in Sir William Berkeley's administrations, 1642-1652, and 1660-1677. On the other hand during the commonwealth period the governor was chosen by the assembly and was subject to removal by that body, and was, therefore, controlled by the assembly. Nevertheless, even in the beginning the Virginia assembly did not meekly submit to the governor in all cases, but showed much independence. The case of Governor Harvey will be recalled. For several reasons, one of which was a refusal of the governor to transmit protests of the assembly on the tobacco question, the council deposed him and elected John West to act as governor until the " king's pleasure " should be known. The king resented this action and sent Harvey back to govern the colony.[1] This act was the act of the council, but it was approved by the burgesses, and when the council called a new assembly and Harvey forbade it to proceed, the prohibition was ignored.[2] Thus both the burgesses and councilors took part in this revolt. The council sent Harvey to England along with the persons to present charges against him and to defend the action of

[1] Doyle, *op. cit.*, i, 198.

[2] *Va. Mag. of Hist.*, i, 422. For documents of the Harvey episode see letters in *MacDonald Pap.*, i, 165, 205.

the assembly. That the Virginians did not intend to assume the power of deposing and electing governors as a right, is indicated by the fact that they chose West to act only until the king's pleasure should be known. The surrender of the colony government to the commission sent by parliament in spite of Governor Berkeley's protest, the subordinate place of the governor during the Commonwealth, and events during Bacon's rebellion furnish other examples of this spirit of independence.

The above seems to briefly describe the situation until after the recall of Governor Berkeley (1677) and the establishment of a two-chambered legislature, when the governor as a member of the upper house began to take a more prominent place in the records. By that time also the legislature had gathered sufficient strength to enter into contests on numerous questions against the governors and their instructions. These facts, along with a series of rather aggressive governors, gave new importance to the relations between the executive and the legislature. With the further development of the legislature during the eighteenth century came more numerous attempts to define and limit the part of the executive in legislating. These attempts culminated in the revolution. Some of the principal relations between the executive and legislature will be seen in the remaining pages of this chapter.

Before 1680 there had been much complaint against governors, and particularly against absentee governors. One of the provisions that was to have been in the proposed charter of 1676, which was almost to the point of being issued, was this, that the governor, council, and other officers should reside in Virginia. News of Bacon's rebellion reached England just in time to prevent the final steps in securing the charter and thus the movement against absentee governors failed. In fact absentee governors were more numerous after than before 1676.

Except during the Commonwealth period and in the absence of a governor, neither branch of the legislature had any control over the appointment of the governor; but the conduct of the legislature or either branch of it might, and sometimes did, influence the length of his term. In fact in the latter part of the seventeenth century the council was successful in driving more than one governor from office.[1] When we remember that the English government frequently considered not fitness but favoritism in its appointments, it is little to be wondered at that there was friction. For example the Earl of Orkney was governor from 1704 to 1737 without ever going to Virginia, and " enjoyed a considerable revenue without performing one act of government."[2] He was represented by a lieutenant or deputy governor. Most of these were interested chiefly in making money for themselves, in strengthening the crown and in promoting their own interests. While it must be said that the council was as a rule in harmony with the governors, there were nearly always a few, sometimes a majority, who were opposed to the governor. Doubtless the councilors, like the governors, were sometimes moved by purely selfish motives, but at other times they were truly loyal to the welfare of Virginia.

An important way in which the governor influenced the legislature was in his power over the meeting, prorogation, and dissolution of the assembly. The power to call together the legislature was considered a privilege of the governor throughout the colonial period, but at times, as in

---

[1] Chalmers, *Hist. of Revolt of Am. Col.*, i, 318–19; *Spotswood Letters*, ii, 284–5. Nicholson, Spotswood, etc., were thus treated.

[2] Chalmers, *Hist. of Revolt of Col.*, i, 394.

1659,[1] the assembly directly authorized him to do so. In the time of Governor Harvey an assembly was called " on the petition of many inhabitants," to receive complaints against the governor.[2]   Hening seems to suggest that the council called it, possibly in response to a petition.   In the absence of the governor, the president of the council and his associates called meetings.   Occasionally the assembly adjourned itself to meet at a specific time.   As for instance in October, 1760, the governor offered to let the burgesses decide when was the most convenient time for them to enter upon the regular business of the country.[3]   Occasionally the house adjourned itself for several days without agreement with the council. As a rule however the governor continued to call assemblies until 1775, when, because of the repeated prorogations, it was found necessary to call a convention independent of the governor.[4]

In closing sessions three methods were used.   They might be prorogued by the governor.   This method was used if the governor intended to call the same assembly in another session.   If the governor contemplated no other session of that assembly he dissolved it.   A third method was adjournment by the assembly itself.   A brief account of how these methods were used in closing sessions will now be given.

After 1645, possibly before, it was a very common thing for the assembly to be prorogued by the governor, though it frequently adjourned itself.[5]   The governor's right to

---

[1] Hening, *op. cit.*, i, 493, 517; ii, 179.   [2] *Ibid.*, i, 223; Howe, 58.

[3] *Jour. of Burg.*, 1760, 6.   [4] *Arch. Am.*, *Series* iv, vol. iii, 395.

[5] The records of 1642, 1647, 1648-9, 1658, 1660-1, 1661-2, 1662, 1663, 1666, 1667, 1676, etc., show the house to have adjourned itself.

dissolve the assembly was disputed in 1658 when the assembly arrogated to itself the entire authority of the government. On April 1 of that year the governor and council declared that " for many important causes " the assembly was dissolved. To this the house through its speaker replied that there was no precedent for such a declaration, and that the attempt to dissolve the assembly was illegal. The house, therefore, asked that the order of dissolution be revoked, and voted that if any member left the house, he should be censured as betraying the trust reposed in him by the country. It was declared that all should remain and act as a whole and entire house. A special oath of secrecy, binding the members not to divulge any of the words or actions of fellow members, was then administered to each one. Upon promise of a speedy conclusion of the business of the assembly, the governor and council expressed themselves as being willing to refer the matter in dispute to Cromwell. The house was not satisfied and asked for a revocation of the order of dissolution.

The revocation was issued, but with the express intention of referring the dispute to Cromwell. Still dissatisfied, the house appointed a committee to draw up a vindication of the assembly. The committee reported that by the records it found " the present power of government to reside in such persons as shall be empowered by the burgesses (the representatives of the people) who are not dissolvable by any power now extant in Virginia, but the House of Burgesses." The committee recommended that the same governor remain in office, but that a new council be chosen. The report was adopted, and all former elections of governor and council which were still in effect were declared void. Colonel Samuel Matthews was re-elected governor. It was declared that a new council, consisting of persons to be " nominated and confirmed by the present burgesses convened (with the advice of the Governor)" should be chosen.   Most of the old councilors were re-elected.   To enable the burgesses to carry their point the sheriff of James City was ordered to obey no warrant unless signed by the speaker.   In seeking for "precedent" it seems the committee did not go farther back than to the surrender to the Commonwealth in 1652.   They based their claim to complete control on the agreement with the Parliamentary commissioners.[1]   This all grew out of the dispute over the power of dissolution, and for the time being the assembly was completely victorious.   The next year the right to dissolve the burgesses except on the consent of the major portion of the house was denied to the governor.[2]   This represents pretty truly the situation during the Commonwealth and early restoration period, but sometime after the restoration of the Stuarts, the power to dissolve the assembly was restored to the governor,[3] and he continued to have this power and to use it till July, 1775, when the convention no longer recognizing the governor resumed the power to adjourn itself.[4]

After 1700 new assemblies were not frequently called. Instead, several meetings of the same assembly were held by prorogation from session to session, thus depriving the people of frequent opportunities of choosing new representatives and so, often, causing much dissatisfaction.[5]

The governor frequently dissolved an assembly if it protested against the acts of the king or of the governor.

[1] Hening, *op. cit.*, i, 499–505; Campbell, Charles, *op. cit.*, 238; Hildreth, *op. cit.*, i, 364–5.

[2] Hening, i, 531; Hildreth, i, 366; Howe, *op. cit.*, 67.

[3] See records in Hening, ii.

[4] Nevertheless the assembly occasionally adjourned itself notwithstanding the above general rule.

[5] Campbell, Charles, 412.

Thus Spotswood first prorogued and then dissolved an assembly for perversity in refusing to tax the people for defensive purposes save in its own way. Governor Dinwiddie dissolved one assembly for factiousness, and, in 1774 Governor Dunmore another, for passing resolutions against the Boston Port Bill.

Occasionally an assembly was dissolved by direct order of the king or of the lords of trade. This happened when the assembly was in opposition to the English government.[1] Occasionally the prorogation came in the form of a command from the governor to the assembly to adjourn itself to a certain day named by him.[2] Then the question arose if in the case of such an adjournment the governor could prorogue again or dissolve that assembly without a meeting? Spotswood and the council disagreed on the matter and it was referred to England for answer.[3] Attorney General West in passing on another case, May 27, 1719, decided that the governor had power to act in such cases.[4]

The foregoing is a statement of the practice in the matter of calling and ending meetings of the assembly, and some of the cases of dispute about it. With the power in his hands, it must be evident that the governor might have much control over the work of legislation and even prevent legislation. Naturally then, even when he did not attempt to direct legislation as far as his power would have permitted, the knowledge of its existence must have had much influence on the legislators.

Another way in which the governor exercised legisla-

---

[1] *Dinwiddie Papers*, i, 161.

[2] *Jour. of Coun. as Upper House*, iii, Oct., 1748, 46; Jan., 1764, 13; *Jour. of Burg.*, Oct., 1754, 60; Oct., 1760, 21; Nov., 1769, 136.

[3] *Spotswood Letters*, ii, 289-90.

[4] Chalmers, *Col. Opinions*, 238. This was a West India case, but had general application.

tive power was by the use of the veto. Although he always possessed the veto power, it must be remembered that in the use of this part of his prerogative the governor was guided in a general way by the instructions which he received from the home government. In some cases the instructions had special reference to some particular act or class of acts; but often they were very general in character and thus left the governor much discretion as to the use of the veto.

Before 1685 there seems to have been little dispute over the question of veto. It seems to have been exercised sparingly but the privilege had not disappeared. Naturally the more influence the governor had in the assembly the less need there was for the use of the veto power. This probably accounts for the little prominence given to the veto under the unicameral legislature. But in 1685 the assembly questioned the veto power of the governor. The dispute arose in this way. When Lord Culpeper was sent out as governor in 1682, he was given instructions that almost deprived the assembly of any real power. Laws were not to be proposed by the assembly, but were to be framed by the governor and council, endorsed or modified by the crown, and then sent to the assembly to be enacted into laws. Many other things in the instructions were equally distasteful to the Virginians. So that although Culpeper did not enforce all of these instructions, when he was succeeded by Lord Howard of Effingham in 1684 the assembly was in a mood for opposition. Most of the former instructions had been renewed and when the governor claimed also that he had a right to veto acts at his discretion, the protest of the assembly was made with vigor. Yet the king ordered the assembly censured for its conduct.[1]

---

[1] Doyle, *op. cit.*, i, 264; Hening, *op. cit.*, iii, 40-1.

When Ludwell's charges against Lord Howard, that he tried to enforce laws which had been repealed, were sent home, the king declared that, when a repealing law was rejected, the act which it was intended to repeal was at once revived. It seems that the assemblymen had claimed that, if an act of assembly had repealed another act and later— possibly after some time had elapsed during which the repealing act was supposed to be valid—the executive had vetoed the repealing act, nevertheless the original act, for a time supposed to be repealed, did not revive, but stood repealed the same as though the veto had not been made. This seems absurd, for if true, an act declared void would still have the same effect as though valid.[1] Therefore the king's position seems to have been sound.

Just when the governor secured a veto regardless of direct instructions is not known. But during most of the colonial period he had such a veto. In its use governors, then as now, greatly differed. Both the veto and assent of the governor to acts were subject to another veto by the home government. As a rule, the veto of the home government was used to nullify objectionable laws to which the governor had given assent, or on which the governor had taken no action. Of the first kind we find an instance in 1752, when the governor sent a message to the assembly stating that fifty-seven acts of the assembly had been approved by the home government, but ten had been vetoed. As the governor considered some of the ten very important, he laid them before the assembly[2] and said that he would help explain to the English government the need of some of these acts. In this case the governor saw the acts

---

[1] *McDonald Pap.*, vii, 229; *Randolph Pap.*, iii, 420, 540; Chalmers, *Pol. Ann.*, 359.

[2] *Jour. of Coun. as Upper House*, April, 1752, iii, 55; *Jour. of Burg.*, Feb., 1752, 95–109.

from the assembly's point of view. Some of the vetoed acts concerned the regulation of the importation of convicts, freedom of colonists from a poll tax,[1] payments of obligations in money instead of in tobacco, the grant to vestries of the right to present ministers,[2] a tax on British manufactures brought to Virginia, acts having more than one subject in them, money questions, especially the issue of paper money, and in general acts tending to the disadvantage of trade, especially of British trade, and to a limitation of the prerogative.

Some general rules were also made by the home government which put a limitation on some subjects of legislation. For example every act passed must continue for a period of two years or more, or it was void. This was for the purpose of giving to the king time enough to consider and, if he desired, to veto the act.[3] Acts once repealed or rejected by the home government could not be re-enacted unless the assembly first got the consent of the crown, or attached to the acts a clause suspending them until the king could pass upon them again.

Even when a measure had passed and had met no present objection, its continuance was indefinite, for acts might be left in force for several years and then be rejected. Naturally this power of repeal at indefinite times was very objectionable to the colonial assembly and caused many protests.

In an indirect way the governor had much influence on the legislature through his part in the selection of speaker and his power to nominate and suspend councilors. As long as there was but one house, the governor as a member of that house had a voice in the election of the speaker.

---

[1] Chalmers, *Hist. of Rev.*, ii, 79.   [2] Chalmers, *Col. Opin.*, 53–60.
[3] Palmer, *Cal. of State Pap.*, i, 206.

In 1653 the governor and council objected to a candidate for the speakership and the burgesses then asked the reasons why the governor and council could not join with the burgesses in the selection of a speaker. The candidate was chosen by a plurality vote, but resigned and another was chosen. At all times the speaker had to be confirmed by the governor. In 1758 the governor was instructed to separate the offices of speaker and treasurer, but he did not do so.

In his control over the council the governor had at times almost enough power to dictate legislation. In 1676 authority to suspend the councilors was given to the governor, though he was answerable to the king for his suspensions. Even as early as 1641 Berkeley was authorized to proceed against any councilor at any meeting of six or more councilors.[1] In theory the councilors were appointed by the king; but the appointments were usually made, either directly by the governor, or by the king on the governor's recommendation. Early in the eighteenth century it was determined that there should be at least nine councilors. To make sure of this number the governor was authorized to keep the council up to nine by appointing persons to fill vacancies. After this the number was seldom more than nine, and thus the governor filled most of the vacancies.[2] The governor, having such control over the appointment and tenure of councilors, and having some of the rights of members of the upper house, being commonly its presiding officer, it must be clear, could, if he wished, exercise much influence on that house. As all legislation had

---

[1] *De Jarnette Pap.*, i, 210, (Virginia State Lib.) Berkeley was also given authority to appoint many other officers and, like every executive who has power to fill offices, he had much opportunity to influence assemblymen.

[2] See page 136.

to pass the council as well as the burgesses, it is easy to see how powerful in legislation the governor might become. However, January 8, 1725, West, council for the Board of Trade and Plantations, and afterward Chancellor for Ireland, held that the governor could not vote as a councilor in passing bills when the council sat in its legislative capacity.[1] The enforcement of this decision would tend to make the governor a mere presiding officer, and give him a place not unlike that of our lieutenant governors in our present-day state senates. This declared inability to vote may have been one reason why many of the governors did not attend the sessions of the council and came in only near the end of the session to sign bills. The journals of the council show the governors to have done this much of the time.[2] Another source of influence on legislation was in the governor's appointive power. This was of great importance. All who sought well paying offices or political promotion must have the friendship of the governor. There were many offices for distribution, and councilors and burgesses alike sought these by voting for some pet scheme of the governor. Many burgesses were made sheriffs or given other lucrative offices. Occasionally the governor used this appointing power to free himself from an obnoxious burgess by appointing him sheriff, and, as in England at an earlier time, practically forcing him to accept the office. Later a law was passed prohibiting any burgess accepting the office of sheriff.[3]

The relations between the governor and the assembly varied with the kind of men in the assembly and the character of the governor. Some governors influenced legislation

---

[1] Chalmers, *Col. Opin.*, 238.

[2] See *Jour. of Coun. as Upper House*, session Feb., 1745, etc.

[3] Further references to the abuse of the appointive power occur in another chapter, pages 88, 133.

by usurpation and violence. A considerable number of them assumed a high and mighty way with the assembly and insisted much on prerogative. They tried to control the assembly to suit their own purposes and sometimes sent peremptory orders to it to consider and act upon recommendations made by them; e. g. in November, 1685, Lord Howard of Effingham, the governor, sent a message requiring the house to act on his recommendations so that he could put an end to the session. He had been angered by the inquiry of the house as to what arms had come into his possession since the last assembly and what he had done with them. The governor said that this matter did not concern them as they were the king's arms; he asked that they attend to the things that he had given them to do.[1] Of course it was the business of the governor to remind the burgesses of their duty to obey the king's wishes; and when those wishes were the governor's will also, it gave good ground for insistence. About the same time as the dispute about the arms, the governor asked that the old custom of sending the house committee lists to him be complied with, but the house said that had been the custom only when joint committees were in vogue; but since the two houses were now separate, and the governor had put an end to the old method of legislating, therefore, " they need not put ye Excellency to soe much trouble, as ye tedious presentment of every Committee must needs create." The governor accepted this as final.

Lord Howard also had objections to the wording of some of the acts of the assembly. In 1685 he asked the assembly to repeal all acts making fines payable to the " Publique " which he said is "a name certainly most odious under a Regal Govern^r & that wch doth in name and con-

---

[1] *Jour. of Coun. as Upper House*, i (Nov., 1685), 36–8, 97.

sequence, but little differ in that detestable one (Republick) wch I am very much persuaded you all soe realy abhor, that you will remove anything wch in the least relates to it." The assembly agreed to make fines payable to the king for the future, but said that the old acts could not be repealed.[1] The same governor told the house it was to its shame, that in three weeks' sitting it had not sent him a single bill to sign.

Among the governors who quarreled most with the assembly were Nicholson and Spotswood. Nicholson, as lieutenant governor and governor, was in Virginia from 1690 to 1692 and from 1698 to 1705. He had much trouble with his councilors, who complained much of his brow-beating methods. The council finally secured his recall. He was accused of using arbitrary and absolute methods, and " in short," the councilors said, " all methods are taken to engross all power into his own hands and to render the council insignif Cypher, which," they said, " is a great alteration of government, much to the dissatisfaction of this Country, and as we conceive, very dangerous and unsafe to his ma'ties service."[2]

---

[1] *Jour. of Coun. as Upper House*, i (1685), 5, 46.

[2] *Va. Mag. of Hist.*, iii, 375 *et seq.*, gives the full charges and they are quoted more fully below, as a sample of the complaints made against the governors, though they are harsher than those made against most of the other governors, because they constitute a party document and were designed to remove a man not in harmony with the local politicians who accused him. They said that he called assemblies too often, and at unseasonable times, and exasperated the members by " harsh speeches and irritating propositions."

Under the heading, " His Behaviour in the Upper House of Assembly," they charge as follows:

" I. Whereas that house humbly conceives that they ought to be left to the freedom of their own debates without being swayed and overawed by the Governor's Interposition; he is not only Continually present, but takes upon himself to preside and debate, and state the questions

In general the charges which the council made against Nicholson were to the effect that he did not allow freedom of debate and tried to browbeat the councilors into thinking and acting as he wished, that he even threatened to cut the throats of the members who refused to comply with his wishes, that he refused to put his speeches in writing and changed the minutes to suit himself, that in the courts he was partial to his friends, abusive to others, and recorded judgments which were not approved by a majority of the court, that he made the queen's name cheap by commanding everything, however insignificant, in the queen's name, that he invented scandalous stories about both men and women enemies, called prominent people by vile names and was very profane.[1] Of course these charges are partisan, but if only a few of them were true there was cause enough to ask for Nicholson's recall. There seems to have been some ground for the charges, for the king instructed

and overrule, as if he were still in Council; which the said House takes to be a great encroachment upon their Liberties and privileges.

"II. His usual high, haughty, passionate and abusive way of browbeating, discouraging and threatening all that speak anything contrary to his opinion or designs is another great encroachment on the Liberties of that House.

"III. His endeavoring to beget or feed a bad understanding between the two Houses; his downright interposing and siding sometimes with one House and sometimes with the other, and making entries to that purpose in the Assembly Books we take to be a great Encroachment on the Liberties of both Houses.

"IV. His Closetting of the members and using all the arts of Cajoling and threatening for his own ends, not sticking sometimes to threaten the cutting of their throats and their utter ruin, we take to be another intolerable encroachment on the Liberties of that House.

"V. He makes severall Extemporary rash speeches to both Houses of Assembly, Cajoling or irritating, promising or threatening, which tho' they have great influence in making or marring the business of the Assemblys, yet are never put into writing, nor appear anywhere in the Minutes of either House of Assembly."

[1] *Va. Mag. of Hist.*, iii, 374–8.

Nicholson to allow freedom of debate and vote to the councilors, though later he was authorized to suspend councilors, thus giving him greater control of them. In case of a suspension the governor was required to report the matter to the king with causes, and with the reply of the suspended councilors. [1]

Spotswood also had much trouble with his councilors, a majority of whom under the leadership of the Blair and Ludwell families, endeavored to secure his recall. In turn the governor tried to secure the removal of the councilors. The quarrel was a bitter one, but neither succeeded in removing the other. Spotswood's opinion of the burgesses has already been stated. One of his dissolution speeches, because of its harsh tone, was disapproved by the Board of Trade.

Dinwiddie was another governor who quarreled with the assembly, but he was on good terms with the legislators much of the time. At the beginning of his administration, he showed a disposition to magnify the importance of the legislature. He said, " The Legislature should always be busy; there are grievances to redress, Irregularities to reform, Defects to supply, and Exuberances to cut off. I presume there are some Laws that want Renewal, and probably others that want Amendment. I therefore most earnestly recommend to you the Prosecution of this great work with Diligence and Expedition. Consider what Bills may be proper and necessary, for promoting the public Quiet, and common Interest, by more effectually securing Property, encouraging and extending Commerce, establishing the Peace, Safety, and Regularity of an equitable and well order'd Government. I will assist you, Gentlemen, to the utmost of my Power, in the

---

[1] *Va. Mag. of Hist.*, iv, 50; Palmer, *Cal. of St. Pap.*, i, 16.

Attainment of these desirable Purposes; and you may expect from me every Concession in your Favour, of which my Instructions will admit." [1]

But Dinwiddie did not always speak thus. In fact he soon came to criticise the burgesses very sharply, as did they him. Especially on the fee question the house said that his demands were illegal, arbitrary and contrary to the charter and anyone thereafter paying them "ought to be regarded as a betrayer of the rights of the people." [2] In spite of much bitterness Dinwiddie got along with the assembly fairly well. Because of the great need for money for defense in his administration the assembly generally had an advantage in controversies, and Dinwiddie often had to give way. Moreover the people came to understand their governor somewhat better also. In a letter to John Pownal, Esq., in March, 1755, he said, " as the People are now sensible of their unjust Clamour and Compl'ts ag'st me, I excuse them, and we are now on good Terms, and believe shall rem'n perfectly easy." [3] Nevertheless he was to have many disputes with them yet. In many cases the addresses of Dinwiddie, as well as of other governors, were abusive The house in return was very severe, but ordinarily kept itself within the forms of courtesy better than the governor. The greater courtesy of the house was probably due to discretion more than to inclination.

While these governors had much strife with the assembly, some governors received high praise from the colonial legislators. William Gooch was a favorite with the people. [4] Another favorite was Governor Botetourt. [5]

---

[1] *Jour. of Burg.*, Feb., 1752, 3.

[2] Chalmers, *Hist. of Rev.*, ii, 351; *Dinwiddie Papers*, i, 44-6.

[3] Dinwiddie Papers, ii, 2.   [4] Chalmers, *Hist. of Rev.*, ii, 161, 198.

[5] A letter dated Aug. 1, 1771, from Richard Bland to Thos. Adams

Sometimes the addresses which passed between the governor and the assembly were very frank, yet expressed the existence of the greatest confidence between them. In the greater part of these addresses is found much very tiresome formalism and cant.

The council was originally designed to advise the governor and to be a check upon him. After the governor was given the power of suspending and nominating, the council became largely a tool in the governor's hands. The control of the patronage by the governor strengthened his hold on the councilors.[1] Nevertheless, in spite of the increased control exercised by the governor, when the stamp act and other measures leading to the revolution were up for consideration, we find most of the councilors on the side of the colonists.

During the time in which the clerk of the burgesses, as well as of the council, was appointed by the governor he had an opportunity to manipulate the records if he so wished. In several cases he was accused of doing this. But this appointment gave him a still more important advantage, in that it provided a spy for the governor in each house. There were several instances in which one or the other of the houses tried to take some action and keep it from the governor, but to no purpose. From the time when Robert Beverley was deposed as clerk of the burgesses and another appointed in his place by the governor, all acts of either house were sure to be communicated to the governor.

in England, says that when Gov. Botetourt died in 1770 the assembly expressed the highest praise for him and voted to erect a statue to him, and "to have it executed by the best Statuary in England, that it may be an ornament to our Capital, where it is to be fixed, a lasting and elegant Testimony that this Country will ever pay the most distinguished Regard and Veneration to Governors of Worth and Merit."

[1] Hartwell, Bl. & Chil., *op. cit.*, 32.

From the foregoing it is clear that the governor had an important part to play in legislation. This part was due not only to the place he had as a constitutional part of the assembly, but also to the many opportunities which he possessed and used to influence and to control indirectly the acts of the council and various members of both houses.[1]

[1] Necessarily much is said in other chapters concerning the relation of the governor to legislation. It has not seemed best to repeat it in this chapter.

CHAPTER VII

The Council as a Part of the Legislature

In the discussion of this chapter it is intended to avoid reference to the council in its administrative and judicial capacities. Reference to those, its most important and conspicuous functions, will be made only when they are necessarily connected with its work as a part of the legislature. So far as it applies to the council the same order of topics as used for the house of burgesses will be followed.

Owing to the fact that the governor's council had administrative and judicial functions, it did not cease to exist in that period after the fall of the company in which there was no general assembly. Although not a legislative body, it is probable that the governor and council did much real legislating as a part of their administrative work. When assemblies were called in 1628 and succeeding years, the council became a part of that body. Like that of the governor, however, the legislative work of the council does not stand out prominently until it became a distinct house, somewhere near 1680. Before that time there was no separate journal kept and therefore the acts of the council are merged in the acts of the general assembly. Nevertheless there are some things about the membership, organization, and procedure of the council that are known, even during the period of the unicameral system.

The number of councilors differed at different times. Probably the regular constitutional number was twelve, but for various reasons the actual number might be more or less than this. In 1676, we find that the number was sixteen.[1] In August, 1702, several meetings of the council had but four members in attendance. This does not prove that those were all that held the office, but it indicates that the total number was small. A small attendance was frequent, as evidenced by the fact that there were commonly a quorum to do emergency business, though five were necessary for ordinary occasions. Hartwell, Blair and Chilton in *The Present State of Virginia* (1727)[2] say that, because of the great mortality, many vacancies occurred in the council, frequently hindering business. To remedy this, when the number fell below nine, the governor was given power to choose and swear into the council enough to make nine. After that power was given, the number was not much in excess of nine.[3] As has already been indicated, the appointment of councilors was in the hands of the king. Gradually the king came to depend on the nominations of the governor, and from those nominated the lords of trade sometimes recommended certain ones to the king, who in turn appointed. This method was used in 1756. Some such method was the rule during the eighteenth century.

To the regular councilors must be added the governor who, when present, presided over the council and until 1725 was considered to have a vote on all bills.[4] After that date the governor frequently absented himself until such time as bills were ready for his signature.[5] He then came

---

[1] Hening, *op. cit.*, i, 511.   [2] *Hartwell, Blair & Chilton, op. cit.*, 22.
[3] See page 126.   [4] See page 127.

[5] In 1742 the council refused to let Dinwiddie act with it either as legislator or judge and appealed to the king to exclude him, and the Board of Trade decided against the council because the claim was new. Chalmers, *Hist. of the Revolt*, ii, 199.

in and in the presence of the council signed the measures of which he approved, and did such other things as might be necessary to close up the work of the session.

The persons above mentioned constituted the regular council. There were however some extraordinary or ex-officio members. The crown's superintendent of Indian affairs and surveyor general of customs were generally so included.[1] These persons, however long they were in the council, did not succeed to its presidency in the absence of the governor and lieutenant governor, as did the regular councilors, and therefore they were not recognized as coun-cilors in the same sense as the others were.

In 1693 the king thought the clergy ought to be rep-resented in the council and so by letter he authorized James Blair, President of William and Mary College, and a commissary of the Bishop of London, to be one of the council. Blair was a constant source of trouble, es-pecially to the governor.[2] Governor Andros and his coun-cil tried to get rid of Councilor Blair in 1695, on the ground that a customs act of the English Parliament pro-hibited any save an English, Irish or colonial born person from holding any customs office. Blair was Scotch and as a member of the general court he had some jurisdiction over customs. He was suspended. This was the second suspension for Blair, and in each case he was restored by the English authorities.[3]

The length of term of councilors was not definitely fixed, save once during the Commonwealth (1659) when the as-sembly declared for a life term. This act was soon re-pealed.[4] In general practice the councilor held during the

---

[1] Stokes, *View of Constitution of British Colonies*, 237.

[2] Hartwell, Blair & Chilton, *op. cit.*, 35–6.   [3] *Ibid.*, 37.

[4] Hening, *op. cit.*, i, 517, 537; Hildreth, *op. cit.*, i, 366. The assem-bly assumed the right to choose and to confirm councilors.

king's pleasure, which usually meant for life or good behavior. In the later period the governor might suspend a councilor for good cause.[1]

The qualifications required of councilors were less definitely stated than for burgesses. It is probable that the requirement of 1676, that office holders should have resided in Viriginia three years, did not apply to councilors, for they received their commissions from the crown, and were in that respect on the same basis as the governor, who was not required to have a definite term of residence. In 1705 the assembly recognized that office holders must be natives, residents for three years, or persons commissioned by the crown.[2] This was the rule until 1776. The councilors did not represent any county, or in fact any division of the colony. They might be chosen from anywhere in the colony, yet because they were colonels and the military commanders of the counties, it is probable that they were well distributed to different parts of the colony. The age in this case, as well as for the burgesses, was probably twenty-one.

While the laws do not designate any definite offenses that disqualified a person for the position of councilor, it seems reasonable that the disqualifications in the laws of 1658,[3] and of 1705,[4] applied to the position of councilor as well as to that of burgess. At least any councilor who was proved guilty of these offenses would probably have been dismissed from office. In 1659 the assembly declared that any one who was convicted of a high misdemeanor, of which the assembly was to be the judge, could not be a

---

[1] Hartwell, Blair & Chilton, 22; Stokes, *op. cit.*, 241.

[2] Hening, *op. cit.*, iii, 251-2; *Spotswood Pap.*, ii, 60.

[3] Hening, *op. cit.*, i, 433; see pages 51–52.

[4] *Ibid.*, iii, 250–1; see page 52.

member of the council.[1]   While the assembly did not long continue in control of the selection of councilors, it is probable that their ideas of fitness continued to have weight.

Bruce's statement that a considerable number of those who became members of both houses had come to the colony as indented servants, has already been referred to.[2] Fiske[3] is of the opinion that these were few, and so far as the council is concerned his view seems quite probable. Many of the councilors, and in the eighteenth century almost all of them, were chosen from the wealthy planters and merchants.[4]   Governor Spotswood spoke of the assembly as being composed of "men of narrow fortune and mean understandings," but he had the burgesses chiefly in mind.[5]   This was probably not wholly true even of the burgesses.   Colonel Robert Quary's statement that the councilors were chosen out of the wealthy land holders, and were selected for "wealth, station and loyalty," and constituted the upper or little house of lords, has been referred to before.[6]   There seems little doubt of the truth of this statement.

Indeed the king's instructions to Governor Nicholson (probably 1705) gave the governor power to nominate men to fill the vacancies in the council, but told him "to take care that they were men of estates and abilities and not necessitous nor much in debt, and that they be persons well affected to his Majesty's Government."[7]

From the first it was customary to administer the oaths

---

[1] Hening, *op. cit.*, i, 517; Hildreth, *op. cit.*, i, 366.

[2] Bruce, *Econ. Hist. of Va.*, ii, 44–6; Ballagh, *White Servitude in Va.* (*J. H. U. S.*), 82–3.   See page 53.

[3] Fiske, *Old Va. and Her Neighbors*, ii, 187.

[4] Bruce, ii, 378; Neill, *Virginia Carolorum*, 15.

[5] Ripley, *op. cit.*, 33–4.   [6] See page 54.

[7] *Va. Mag. of Hist.*, iv, 49–50.

of allegiance and supremacy to councilors.[1] This required them to be supporters of the church of England. In such a loyal colony as Virginia it is improbable that any but a churchman could possibly have been a councilor. Catholics were prohibited from holding any office, and at various times, so were Quakers and other nonconformists.[2]

We have seen [3] that the burgesses were very insistent that a burgess should not hold other offices; it was not so with councilors. Indeed the councilors held almost any of the important offices save those of burgess and sheriff. They were the supreme judges, collectors, naval officers, colonels and commanders in chief of counties, escheators, farmers of quit rents, and were charged with the execution of the revenue laws.[4] In general they received appointment to the places of greatest responsibility and profit.

The officers of the council were few. When present the governor presided,[5] but as the governor was frequently, and in the eighteenth century generally, absent from the meetings, a president of the council was necessary. This office was held by that councilor who had earliest taken the oath of office. Besides his regular duty as presiding officer of the council, he with the council was to administer the government during such intervals as might occur between the death of one governor and the appointment of another.[6]

Sometimes when the governor was intending to be absent, he commissioned the president of the council to act as governor during his absence.[7]

Another officer of the council was the clerk. He also

---

[1] See page 55.   [2] See references pp. 55–56.
[3] See pages 56–58.   [4] Hartwell, Blair & Chilton, 24, 32.
[5] *Dinwiddie, Pap.*, i, 42.   [6] Beverley, bk. iv, 2.
[7] *Jour. of Coun. as Upper House*, ii, 1 (1746).

acted as clerk of the general assembly when the two houses were in joint session. Because of this fact considerable confusion is found in the records in the use of terms, especially as has been said before,[1] in the use of the term " clerk of the assembly." The terms " clerk of the assembly " and " clerk of the council " are found used interchangeably just as are the terms " clerk of the house " and " clerk of burgesses," which were in truth two terms referring to the same officer.[2] After 1686 the governor appointed the clerk of the burgesses in the presence of the council in the council chamber.[3] Probably the clerk of the council was also appointed in about the same way.[4] The only other officer was a door-keeper chosen by the council and paid by appropriations from the general treasury.

The privileges and immunities of councilors, while in some respects similar to those of the burgesses, differed quite essentially. Though the laws regarding the arrest of legislators do not as a rule refer to councilors, there is no doubt that councilors were exempt from arrest to even a greater degree than burgesses. The law of 1664 providing that no arrest be made at James City between five days before and five days after sessions of the general court and of the assembly, unless the persons resided in the county of James City, was general in its application and protected councilors as well as burgesses.[5] In addition to this the councilors claimed exemption from ordinary writ of arrest at all times; but it was ordered that on letter of summons signed by the governor or secretary they must attend

---

[1] See pages 84–85.

[2] *Jour. of Coun. as Upper House*, i, 57, 65 (Nov., 1685).

[3] *Ibid.* (Aug., 1702), 2–3; *Jour. of Burg.*, May, 1740, 1.

[4] Palmer, *op. cit.*, i, 93 (Oct., 1705).   [5] Hen., ii, 213.

court and, in case of failure to do so, they were subject to the ordinary forms of common process.[1]

Ordinarily the councilors took rank among themselves according to the order of taking the oath of office and not according to the time of appointment. This sometimes led to disputes over privilege, as was the case in 1756, when Philip Ludwell and William Beverley each claimed precedence over the other.[2]

The assembly of 1639-40 exempted the councilors and ten servants of each from public taxes; but this was repealed four years later. However, the instructions of Charles I to Governor Berkeley, 1642, state that, as part of the pay of councilors they and ten servants each were to be exempt from all public charges and contributions levied by the assembly, save for defensive war, assistance toward building a town or churches, or minister's dues.[3] In 1658 the act of 1639-40 was renewed, except as regards church duties.[4] In the eighteenth century tax exemption for councilors does not appear in the laws, and from the fact that it became customary to pay them salaries in money it is possible, though hardly likely, that this exemption was withdrawn.

Councilors were protected from slander by a provision of law that any one who was guilty of such an act should be imprisoned. Judging from a case in 1658[5] the burgesses

[1] *Va. Mag. of Hist.*, iv, 51. This is taken from instructions to Gov. Nicholson.

[2] *Dinwiddie, Pap.*, ii, 350-1.

[3] *Va. Mag. of Hist.*, ii, 283; also *Robinson MSS.*, 227. (Va. Hist. Soc. Lib.)

[4] Hening, *op. cit.*, i, 445.

[5] In 1658 Solomon Martin, for scandalously asserting that Col. Wm. Bernard, a member of the council, could make his servants swear what he wished, was imprisoned for a few days. Hening, i, 515.

imposed the penalty, but it is not likely that they did so after they were deprived of judicial power.

Punishment of councilors was usually in the hands of the governor, or of the governor and other councilors jointly. The instructions to Governor Berkeley (1641) authorized him to proceed against any councilor at any meeting at which six or more councilors were present.[1] In the period of usurpation during the Commonwealth the burgesses assumed the right to expel councilors.[2] In 1676 power to suspend the councilors was given to the governor alone, but with the proviso that he should give substantial reasons therefor, and be answerable to the king for the truth of the accusations.[3] During the suspension the councilor could not be a member of the assembly. This authority to suspend was given to the governor because it was said that Bacon's rebellion might have been prevented if the governor had possessed the power to suspend at the beginning of that disturbance.[4]

Though the governor was supposed to suspend only for cause, it is possible that he was occasionally tempted to see cause where little or none existed. At least Lord Howard of Effingham was charged by his enemies in the colony with suspending because of personal dislike and even with imprisoning councilors without making any charge against them.[5] Governor Spotswood complained of the opposition of his council and asked that he be given one that he could work with,[6] but he could not suspend all the members on the ground of mere opposition. The reasons for the suspension of a councilor were to be reported to the king and

---

[1] *De Jarnette Pap.*, i, 210, (Va. St. Lib.)   [2] Hildreth, i, 366.

[3] Beverley, bk. iv, 2.   [4] Hartwell, Bl. & Chil., 23.

[5] See Ludwell's charges as given in *McDonald Pap.*, vii, 236.

[6] *Spotswood Pap.*, ii, 284–5; see p. 131.

to the committee of trade and plantations.[1] When Governor Andros tried to get rid of Commissary Blair, by suspending him, the king restored him and said that he was to remain in the council until he, the king, thought he had forfeited his seat; thus the suspension was overruled. Nevertheless, on a new charge, Blair was soon suspended again, and again restored.[2] He was a rather aggressive opponent of several of the governors. In January, 1719, William Byrd was by order of the lords of trade restored to the council. He had been excluded by reason of long absence. In 1756 Lewis Burwell, president of the council, having absented himself for a long time and sending no excuse, was considered to have forfeited his seat.[3]

The salaries of councilors were not definitely provided for at first. Before the time of Governor Culpeper, 1680-3, the councilors had received no pay except exemption from taxes already referred to,[4] and allowances for accommodations at Jamestown while attending to public business;[5] but during his administration began the custom of paying them a small amount. The " Lord President " received 500 pounds sterling.[6] However, Beverley (1705) says that " the salary of the Council is in all but 350£ per annum to be proportioned among them according to their Attendance on General Courts, and Assemblies." [7] In Governor Gooch's term it is said that this was increased to £600.[8] This was paid by appropriating money from the general

---

[1] *Va. Mag. of Hist.*, iv, 49–50.

[2] Hartwell, Bl. & Chil., 35–6; see page 137.

[3] *Dinwid. Pap.*, ii, 374; *Va. Mag. Hist.*, iv, 50.

[4] See p. 142.   [5] Hening, *op. cit.*, i, 423, 498, 523; ii, 359.

[6] Ripley, *op. cit.*, 101.

[7] Beverley, *op. cit.*, bk. iv, 5–6; Hartwell, Bl. & Chil., *op. cit.*, 34.

[8] *Va. Mag. of Hist.*, iii, 117.

treasury, as in the case of burgesses. Governor Spotswood thought this a dangerous custom and tried to prevent it. In a letter to the committee of trade, 1711, he said that he had not suffered the method of paying salaries to councilors to continue, as it tended to destroy the dependence they ought to have on the crown; that they ought to depend on the crown for support.[1] He did not succeed in making entire dependence on the crown permanent, and later are found several instances showing that even the governor received pay from the burgesses.[2]

The salaries of officers of the council, like those of the other house, varied much. In 1754 the clerk of the general assembly received £30; in 1765, £80; the doorkeeper £5 and £15 at the corresponding times. At other times the salaries were usually somewhere between these two amounts.

Sessions of the council, like those of the English upper house, were usually much shorter than those of the lower house. They usually began at 10 or 11 a. m., and there are few references to afternoon sessions. In the latter part of May, 1706, however, the council met at 8 or 9 a. m. The slight amount of business recorded shows little need of long sessions. When the council allowed all the business to originate in the lower house, it had much less to do. It met and adjourned from day to day or even from week to week until the burgesses brought up some bills to them.

The methods of doing business in the council have already been referred to in part in connection with the burgesses.[3] Ordinarily then, the forms of procedure of the two houses differed little, except that committees were not

---

[1] *Spotswood, Letters*, i, 49.

[2] Hartwell, Bl. & Chil., 31; *Jour. of Coun. as Upper House*, iii, 117; *Jour. of Burg.*, Feb., 1745, 118.

[3] See p. 110.

much used in the council, the whole body acting together on all questions. During conferences with the other house, however, the committee was always in use.

About 1742 the council got in the habit of doing business in a hurry. Bills were given three readings in close succession and were passed without much apparent consideration. They also left the initiation of business to the burgesses. Consequently in the early part of the session their chief business was to meet and to adjourn to the next day or to the next week.[1]

The relations of the council to the house of burgesses give much insight into real legislative conditions in the colony. It will be recalled that before the separation of the two houses both the council and burgesses occasionally attempted to act separately, as when the council refused to join with the burgesses in the choice of Lieutenant Colonel Chile as speaker in 1653, and, when the burgesses dismissed the governor and council for attempting to dissolve the assembly in 1658. During that same period it will be recalled that the burgesses assumed the power to elect and to dismiss councilors at will. In 1667 the burgesses declined to allow the council to take part in the making up of the tax levy.

After the complete separation of the two houses there was a tendency to develop different functions. A spirit of jealousy was also developed which occasionally became almost enmity. This had some important consequences in connection with the efforts of the burgesses to gather power into their own hands.

As has before been noted, during at least a part of the time the council left the initiation of most of the legislation to the lower house and thereby became what the English

---

[1] *Jour. of Coun. as Upper House*, May, 1742, 11-14, 53; Feb., 1752, 1; May, 1765, 1.

upper house is today, a check upon the people's representatives. All petitions were referred by the council to the burgesses for their action. Yet the council was at times as active as the other house in legislating.[1] Chalmers seemed to think that the council, with its various functions, had such a place in the government that it was almost absolute.[2] This does not seem to be true for all times, but their small number, their more permanent tenure of office, and their other powers, gave the councilors a place distinct from that occupied by the burgesses.

Some of the practices of the two houses seem to imply that the burgesses recognized their house as inferior to the council. The following points will illustrate this. When the two houses came together in joint session it was the house that went to the council in the council chamber. It is probable that the clerk of the council was the clerk of the joint meeting, that is, of the general assembly met in one body.[3] In transmitting messages and bills the council sent their clerk; the burgesses sent a committee of its own members.[4] When new burgesses were chosen the councilors administered the oath of office to them.[5] These practices might well be considered sufficient to indicate that the council had the superior place in the legislature.

And yet the burgesses were chosen by the people and held authority directly from the people, while the council was chosen by the royal power and had less direct connections with the people. It was but natural, therefore, that jealousies should arise between the two houses and that

---

[1] *Jour. of Coun. as Upper House* (Apr., 1704), 1–2, 12, etc.

[2] Chalmers, *Hist. of Rev.*, i, 317.

[3] *Jour. of Coun. as Upper House*, i, 74 (Nov., 1685).

[4] *Ibid.*, ii (Apr., 1706), etc. This seems to be what was proposed on the organization of Congress under the constitution of 1789.

[5] See p. 101.

the one, because of its superior social and political position, and the other, because of its nearness to the people, should each try to gain an advantage over the other. Doubtless the governor tried to create and keep up dissension between the two houses for his advantage.[1] While both houses were at times somewhat aggressive and each inclined to encroach upon the other, the house of burgesses seems to have been the worse offender in this direction. The fact that the originating of money bills was considered as belonging to the burgesses gave them great power and enabled them to enforce their demands in cases where money was involved. It was a general policy with the burgesses to enforce their position by withholding appropriations. This is further discussed in the next chapter.[2]

A few illustrations of disputes between the two houses will readily show the feeling of jealousy which existed between them, and at the same time show some of the efforts of each house to gain an advantage over the other.

The attempt of the council to prevent the payment of a salary to the speaker of the house has been referred to before.[3]

In 1714 a dispute arose as to who should present to the governor an address to the king congratulating him on his accession. After several conferences it was agreed that if the governor received it in the council chamber the councilors were to stand and the speaker of the house should present it; but if he received it in " the pallace," i. e. the governor's residence, the oldest councilor was to present it. The governor decided to receive it in the council chamber.[4]

In October, 1744, six burgesses and three councilors

---

[1] Council charges against Gov. Nicholson, *Va. Mag. of Hist.*, iii, 377. See p. 130; note iii.

[2] See pp. 163–165.   [3] See pp. 98–99.

[4] *Jour. of Coun.*, ii, 11 (Nov., 1714).

were holding a conference on a fee bill; one of the councilors contrary to all precedent put on his hat during the meeting and read a paper. The house took this as an offense and asked the council if its representative acted under directions of the council, and if the council claimed it as a right that its conference managers should sit with hats on in conference while the burgesses remained uncovered. The burgesses refused to receive the paper read at the conference until an answer was received from the council. The council sent answer that no offense was intended and that the councilor had expected others to put on their hats when he had done so. The house accepted the explanation as satisfactory.[1]

Another dispute arose over the question of removing the capital in 1748. The two houses were on opposite sides, the burgesses favoring the removal. John Blair, a councilor, while talking to a burgess, pointed to the speaker of the house who was passing and said, " There goes the man who is at the bottom of this H—— Scheme and has told several Lies and advanced many Things that he knew to be false and therefore he had no Confidence in such a Man, that his only motive is his private Interest though he pretends the publick Good." The burgesses said this reflected on the honor of both the speaker and the house and resolved to bring charges against Blair and ask the council to punish him. The council inquired into the matter, Blair confessed and excused himself because of a " warm temper." A message was sent to the house explaining the situation and asking that this affair should not interfere with public business. This action was accepted as satisfactory.[2]

---

[1] *Jour. of Coun. as Upper House*, ii, 58 *et seq.* (Sep., 1744); *Jour. of Burg.*, Sep., 1744, 76.

[2] *Jour. of Coun. as Upper House*, iii, 17–8 (Nov., 1748); *Jour. of Burg.*, Nov., 1748, 41–2.

In 1748-9 a serious dispute arose as to whether the burgesses had the right to search the journals of the council without its leave. The house appointed some of its members to make such search and no permission was asked. The council ordered its clerk to refuse such privilege unless a message should come from the house to the council asking for such permission. This act of the burgesses seems to have been an effort to control the entire government in the interest of the popular party.[1] It is, however, only one of several evidences of bad feeling at this time. On March 23, the burgesses sent a written message to the council that, as it was the season of the year (Easter) which was generally given over to religion, and as they knew of no reason why public business could not be interrupted, they would use " their undoubted Right " to adjourn from Thursday to Monday; they hoped the councilors, being good churchmen, would do the same. At first the council laid the message on the table, then ordered it expunged from the records and adjourned till Saturday. The cause of this failure to agree on adjournment, and of the rather radical and aggressive acts of the two houses is not very clear in the records, but was probably factiousness growing out of disputes on other questions.

The council then again took up the claim of the house that it had the right to search the council journal without permission. In the meantime it seems that the burgesses had passed a resolution stating that the council had violated an " undoubted Right and Privilege of their House." This resolution would be published in the journal and spread abroad at the close of the session. Therefore the council, to defend itself, prepared and passed some resolutions in

---

[1] *Jour. of Coun. as Upper House*, iii, 7, 19, 21 *et seq.*, 91, 106, 114–20; Palmer, *op. cit.*, i, lxiii, 241.

answer to that of the house.   These resolutions stated that the regular method of getting information was by one house addressing the other asking for it.   " But since the Burgesses have presum'd to run counter to this ancient, decent, and established Method,—the Council find themselves under the unpleasing Necessity of publickly vindicating the Legality of their Proceedings, which has been reflected upon with such mistaken Heat, and unparallel'd Severity." They resolved to print their defense in the *Virginia Gazette,* a paper published by the public printer.   Some of the burgesses told the printer that he would be taken into custody and deprived of his position, if he printed the resolutions. The paper appeared without the resolutions and Parks, the publisher, was called before the council to explain.   He said that the governor had ordered him to delay the publication for at least a week.   The council then prepared an address to the governor, asking if he had given such an order and, if so, upon whose advice.   If he had given such an order, he was asked to revoke it.   It was on March 27 that Parks was ordered to print the resolutions.   He finally did so on May 10, and sent his submission to the council. On May 11, the burgesses ordered Parks into custody and sent a message to the council, asking if it had prepared the resolutions.   They said that the methods were so unparliamentary and so beneath the character assumed by the council, that they would not believe the council had ordered the resolutions printed.   The council replied in rather violent language, that it had given the order.   The governor now called for the bills that were ready for his signature, made his farewell address after 22 years as governor, and closed the assembly.   This was probably the most violent of all the quarrels between the two houses and was due to the efforts of the house to assume too much power and to dominate the government.   Other instances of like character may be referred to very briefly. In 1706, when the governor was urging military preparations, the council was frequently with him against the burgesses. Conferences having as their object the settlement of differences between the two houses were very frequent on both military and other matters.[1] In 1740 the burgesses prepared an address to the king and a petition to the Commons to give Virginia the same liberty of importing salt as was possessed by northern colonies. The council refused to join in the address and petition. The burgesses then resolved to appoint Edward Randolph as agent to secure the thing desired. The council refused to agree to the appointment.[2] Later the burgesses succeeded in another similar move. The Ludwell[3] Papers show that the council complained to the burgesses that the lower house had assumed to itself complete control over complaints and grievances sent to the general assembly. The council said that they should come before the governor and council as well as the burgesses. The burgesses sometimes attached riders to money bills to gain their point.[4] As early as 1740 the attempt of the burgesses to appoint an agent in England was a cause of dispute between the two houses.

Still other incidents tend to illustrate the relations existing between the two houses, such as disputes over taxation, over judicial appeals to the assembly, etc., but they add little that is new.[5]

---

[1] *Jour. of Coun. as Upper House*, i, 49–50, 53, 57–59.

[2] *Ibid.*, ii, 3–4 (Aug. 21, 1740).

[3] *Ludwell Papers* (MSS.), ii, no. 34.

[4] *Jour. of Burg.*, Aug., 1754, 18.

[5] Disputes over pay to Ludwell, *Va. Mag. of Hist.*, v, 63; on questions of appeals, Hartwell, Blair & Chilton, *op. cit.*, 26; on taxes, Hartwell, Bl. & Chil., *op. cit.*, 62; on search of Council Journal, *Calendar Va. St. Pap.*, i, 241, etc.

In all these disputes, as well as in all disagreements over bills, resolutions, addresses, and the like, the common procedure was a conference. There was a special room set apart for this work and the house usually had twice as many representatives as did the council. While there were frequent instances of failure to agree, some compromise was reached in the majority of cases. Occasionally terms of a conference could not be agreed upon.[1]

From what has thus far been given it might seem that the customary relations between the houses were hostile. This is hardly true, for these cases involve only one side, and are given because they represent phases of the legislature that could be presented in no other way. The fact that a great deal of legislating was done and much of it without friction, the fact that in many cases the two houses united in addresses both of opposition and approval of the governor and of the English government, shows that while the rivalry usually existing between the two houses may have been present, it did not prevent the real work of legislation.

[1] *Jour. of Coun. as Upper House*, ii (March, 1747), 24–5.

CHAPTER VIII

Features of the Legislature as a Whole

This chapter will include some discussion of such topics
as the place of meeting of the legislature, petitions to the
legislature, control of money questions, appointment and
administration, judicial business, treaties, and the establishment of two houses.

The place of meeting of the legislature remained at Jamestown throughout the seventeenth century, with the exception
of two sessions. These were the ones following Bacon's
rebellion, when, because the state house had been destroyed,[1]
one session was held at Green Spring, the home of Governor Berkeley, and one at Middle Plantation.

In December, 1700, the sessions were held in the college
building adjoining Williamsburg. This continued to be
the meeting-place until 1705, when a state house was built
at Williamsburg. There seems to have been no dispute over
the removal from Jamestown, the governor and both houses
agreeing to the change.[2] But the state house at Williamsburg having been burned, the session of July, 1746, was en-
livened by a disagreement of the two houses on the question
of rebuilding or removing to another place. A conference
failed to settle the matter and it went over to the next session.[3] In October, 1748, the act to rebuild at Williamsburg

[1] Hening, *op. cit.*, ii, 401.

[2] Palmer, *op. cit.*, i, 75.

[3] *Jour. of Coun. as Upper House*, ii (July, 1746), 28; (Oct., 1748), 49.

became a law, although with much opposition.[1]   This
is evident from the fact that in the next session in
April, a bill to establish a new town near Newcastle and
to build at private expense buildings for public use, was
passed by the burgesses, (probably by a two-thirds vote) but
was defeated by the council.   John Robinson, Thomas Lee
and William Fairfax of the council favored the measure.
They said that two-thirds of the people favored removal.[2]

Again, in 1752, the burgesses passed an act to establish a
town to become the capital, by a vote of 44 to 34, but the
council refused to pass it to a second reading.[3]   In the meantime the state house was being rebuilt at Williamsburg and
both houses passed appropriations to pay the builder.[4]   In
1761 the burgesses rejected a bill to remove the capital by
a vote of 35 to 36.[5]   The matter again came up in 1772
and a resolution that a bill for removal be prepared was
carried by the burgesses by a vote of 34 to 25.[6]   After
much parliamentary skirmishing the bill finally passed by
a vote of 48 to 32.[7]   However, the capital remained at Williamsburg until the revolution.   The conventions of July
and December, 1775 met in Richmond but the latter adjourned to meet at Williamsburg.   It was at Williamsburg
that the convention met to adopt the first state constitution.

The right of petition to the assembly was early recognized.   Although used in the case of Governor Harvey, in
1635, it was probably not directly authorized and provided for before 1664.   It was then provided that notice
of meetings of the assembly should be given in the parish

---

[1] *Jour. of Coun. as Upper House*, iii (Oct., 1748), 23–41; Hen., vi, 197–8;
(Oct., 1748), 49–54. Dispute over this has already been referred to on
p. 149.   [2] *Jour. of Coun.*, iii (Mar., 1748–9), 56–7.

[3] *Ibid.* (Feb., 1752), 65; *Jour. of Burg.*, Feb., 1752, 70, 71, 93, 99.

[4] *Jour. of Coun.* (Nov., 1753), 30. [5] *Jour. of Burg.*, March, 1761, 84.

[6] *Ibid.*, 1772, 42.   [7] *Ibid.*, 1772, 89, 97, 100, 103, 116.

churches and that days should be appointed for the people to meet in their election places and present their grievances to the burgesses. This was a legal provision for petitions to the government for redress of those grievances.[1] This law gave rise to all sorts of complaints and unsigned petitions which did more evil than good. It was amended in June, 1680, and by the amended act the sheriff was to appoint a time and place for the meeting and all petitions had to be signed, or they could not be presented in the assembly.[2] The right to petition continued throughout the colonial era, and was much used. Occasionally, however, near the end of a session a limit was put to the time at which petitions would be received. This was only to prevent their coming in during the last few days of the session, when there was no time to act upon them. The enactment of 1680 was re-newed in 1705 and again was re-enacted in 1762 under the head of a provision for a court of claims in each county, where claims, grievances, and petitions to the assembly might be presented.[3] Claims against the colony were brought in this way, and the house refused to allow them to be brought otherwise.[4] When the petition was received, it was referred to the proper committee and acted on as was other committee business. The subjects of petition were many; as petitions for office, for pay for slaves killed while in outlawry or while being punished, for pay for tobacco destroyed by fire and flood while in public warehouses, against inoculation for small-pox, for reward for discover-ing a cure of some disease. Petitions for permission to es-tablish roads, bridges and ferries both at public and private expense, were numerous. The organist at Williamsburg

---

[1] Hening., *op. cit.*, ii, 211-2.   [2] *Ibid.*, 482.

[3] Hening, *op. cit.*, vii, 528; Hartwell, Blair & Chilton, 38.

[4] *Jour. of Coun. as Upper House* (Nov., 1685), i, 11-13.

church, the public printer, and the jailor, usually had to petition not only for an increase of salary, but for continuance
of the regular allowance.   In fact it is hard to think of any
subject which was not occasionally represented by a petition.
Of this system, as worked out, it is said " to know the
Pressures, Humours, common Talk, and Designs of the
People of that Country, perhaps there is no better Way than
to peruse the Journals of the House of Burgesses, and of
the Committee of Grievances and Propositions, which is
one of the Committees of that House." [1]

The control of money affairs, including taxation and
appropriations, was a matter of great importance in the
colonial legislature of Virginia.   Around the questions of
where the control should be, and how and when it should
be exercised, centre many of the quarrels between the two
houses, between the assembly and the governor, and between the colonists and the home government.   Control
over taxation will first be discussed.

It will be remembered that the assembly of 1619 levied
a tax of one pound of tobacco per poll to pay its officers,
but made no further claim in regard to taxation; also that
in 1623 the assembly forbade the governor to lay any taxes
which were not authorized by the assembly.[2]   In 1629 the
assembly exercised authority over these things and levied
a tax of five pounds of tobacco " per pol," and appropriated it for certain specified expenditures, which, for the
most part, had already been made.[3]   It also provided a
detailed system of collection, the burgesses being the col-

---

[1] Hartwell, Blair & Chilton, *op. cit.*, 39.

[2] See pp. 25, 29. Hening, *op. cit.*, i, 124. Chalmers (*Pol. Ann.*), 64,
says that in 1624 was the first participation of the assembly in power of
taxation.   This is not quite true, as it is shown above that the assembly
of 1619 levied a tax.

[3] Hening, *op. cit.*, i, 142.

lectors. The assembly of 1631-2 again asserted complete control over taxes and appropriations.[1] This was confirmed in September of the same year, in 1634, and again in 1645. The terms of the surrender of 1652 contained a declaration that Virginia was " free from all taxes, customs and impositions whatsoever, and none to be imposed on them without consent of the Grand Assembly." Shortly after the restoration the assembly gave to the governor and council power to levy taxes for three years, to pay debts and salaries allowed by the assembly and such other debts as the executive council should find justly due; but this tax might not amount to more than twenty pounds of tobacco per poll in any one year. The object in giving such authority was to remove the necessity of an annual meeting of the assembly when it had little or no other business to do.[2] This did not grant full power to levy taxes; nevertheless in those times it was a very dangerous authority to confer upon an executive body.

In November, 1666, the governor desired that two or more of the council might join with the burgesses in making the tax levy, but the burgesses refused to allow it, and insisted upon the privilege of laying the tax in the house of burgesses, and upon leaving to the governor and council only the privilege of approving or disapproving the levy thus made. The acceptance of this arrangement by the governor and council as a guide for the future [3] seems to show that the laying of the tax levy had already been taken from the whole assembly and given to the burgesses alone, though the right to ratify or reject was left in the hands of the other portion of the assembly. It is impos-

[1] Hening, *op. cit.*, i, 171.

[2] *Ibid.*, ii, 24; Campbell, C., 254; *Session Acts*, 1661–2, 33.

[3] Hening, *op. cit.*, ii, 254; *Randolph MSS.*, 303 (Va. Hist. Soc. Lib.).

sible to say that this was always the method pursued, but there is little doubt that it was the method aimed at by the burgesses. There are a number of declarations at different dates to show that this was the ideal. For example, in the arguments of the London agent of the assembly about 1675, it was said that the kings had never offered to impose any tax upon Virginia without the consent of their subjects there.[1] Again, in 1676, this right was asserted. In a resolution of May, 1769, the house declared that the sole right of imposing taxes belonged to the burgesses.[2] The protest against the Stamp Act was of the same nature.[3] The same sentiment is expressed also in the letter of Governor Gooch to the Lords of Trade in which he said that all bills for laying taxes on the people take rise in the house of burgesses, and generally all bills prepared on petition or representation of the people are first moved there, but either house may frame bills.[4] The same governor again recognized this in 1740, when he said that the Lords of Trade would question the duty on slaves which is assessed on the buyer, but that " the people's representatives " think no other tax can be levied.[5] Keith makes reference to the fact that the burgesses resisted every effort of the governor, or of the governor and council, to levy taxes or to collect fees not authorized by them.[6] Although the burgesses claimed almost complete control over taxation they were not averse to permitting the English government occasionally to suggest measures of taxation, though they still held the right to accept or reject the suggestions. In 1680 Charles II

---

[1] Hening, ii, 526.   [2] *Jour. of Burg.* (May, 1769), 37.

[3] *Ibid.* (Oct., 1764), 37-8.

[4] Gooch was governor from 1727 to 1749. See his letter printed in *Va. Mag. of Hist.*, iii, 114-17.

[5] *Jour. of Coun. as Upper House* (May, 1740), 3.

[6] Keith, *op. cit.*, 167; *Va. Mag. of Hist.*, i, 176.

sent over by Lord Culpeper four bills which, when passed by the assembly, were to become law. One of these was a renewal of the act of 1661 imposing two shillings per hogshead on tobacco exported from Virginia, but omitting that part which put an export tax of ten shillings on ships not bound for an English port. The acts of 1661 [1] had exempted ships owned wholly by inhabitants of Virginia from these export duties, and an act of 1669 [2] had exempted such vessels from the castle duties of one half pound of powder and three pounds of shot per ton burden of the vessel or one shilling in money in lieu thereof, and six pence for each passenger. Now the bill sent over by the king called for the two shillings tax and a renewal of the castle duties and made no exemption for Virginia owners. The burgesses rejected the measure; but, when it was amended by such exemptions as had prevailed before, they finally passed it. [3] The revenue from this act was made a permanent fund for the use of the government and was largely under the control of the governor. To some degree this lessened the power of the assembly and increased that of the governor.

Although the assembly was so careful to keep control of taxation, it was not equally careful to use that control justly. When the great landowners dominated the assembly, as they did much of the time, it levied a poll rather than a land tax, and thus put an unjust share of the burden on the poorer classes. At times the councilors seemed more inclined to be just than the burgesses, for in 1683 they recommended the abolition of poll taxes, and the substitution

---

[1] Hening, ii, 130-2, 133-4, 135-6.　　[2] *Ibid.*, 272.

[3] *Ibid.*, ii, 466, and note. Chalmers seems to give the idea that the exemption was in the bill as sent by the king. He says the bill was disapproved by the Lords of Trade. Chalmers, *Pol. Ann.*, 341-2, 354.

of a tobacco tax which would have borne more heavily on the wealthy landowner than on the poor, and would have been more nearly according to the principle of ability to pay. It was not adopted.

Hartwell, Blair and Chilton say that the assembly in levying a tax first found the whole charges against the country, added eight per cent for cost of casks for the tobacco paid in, and ten per cent for cost of collection, and divided this equally among the tithables, i. e. slaves of both sexes, and males over sixteen years of age. Other taxes, on trade and lands, were sometimes levied, but generally for some specific purpose.[1]

Tax laws giving special advantages to Virginians, even as against Englishmen, such as the exemption acts of 1661 and 1680 above mentioned, were not uncommon in the colony. The object was to encourage ship building and ship owning by inhabitants of the colony. These laws seem to have been endeavoring to do for Virginia much the same thing as England was then trying to do for English merchants and shipowners by means of the navigation acts. When money was wanted for the war in 1710, the Virginia assembly proposed to raise £20,000 on British manufactures and on British merchants doing business in the colony.[2]

We thus see that the control of taxation was clearly in the hands of the assembly, usually of the burgesses, during the whole period of their legislative existence. Where did it get this authority? Not from any direct grant of the power, for no such grant was ever made. Chalmers says that it came from the possession of property.[3] The pos-

---

[1] Hartwell, Blair & Chilton, *op. cit.*, 54.

[2] Chalmers, *Hist. of Rev.*, i, 396; *Spotswood, Letters*, introd., ix, 129-33.

[3] Chalmers, *Pol. Ann.*, 55.

session of property doubtless forced its possessors to take control of taxation in order that they might protect that property. Moreover it is the history of English peoples that the representatives of the people ultimately gain control of the power to tax the people.

The next topic that comes up for consideration is the control over appropriations. In the early history of the colony the right of the assembly to make appropriations was not an exclusive one. Sometimes and for some objects the executive council decided the matter. Gradually the assembly extended its power over a wider ranger of appropriations, and as "the assembly" came more and more to mean the burgesses, the control of the executive council slowly became less and less. By the end of the seventeenth century the control of appropriations was in the hands of the assembly and to a considerable degree in the lower house, and so remained till the revolution. An exception was in the control over appropriations for the salaries of the governor and secretary. These were the king's officers and were paid out of the king's revenues. To allow the assembly to control these might have given it too much influence over the king's officers and made them dependent upon the legislature instead of upon the king. Even the councilors were sometimes paid out of the king's revenue for the same reason. To prevent any undue influence over the royal officials the instructions to Effingham forbade the legislature making any appropriation for the governor, deputy, or council, unless the money was given to the use of the king. The act provided that the money was to remain in the treasury until the king signified his consent for the officers to have it. The act also indicated how the money should be used if the king did not consent.[1] There are a

----

[1] *Randolph Pap.*, iii, 436.

few exceptions to this rule however.　Because of the troubled times in England in 1643, the governor's salary was cut off.　To enable him to support the dignity of his office the assembly levied a special tax and made an appropriation for his benefit.　Great care was taken that, (since this was the first time in the history of the colony that money was appropriated for such a purpose), it should not become a precedent, but be simply an accommodation to the governor.[1]　During the Commonwealth the governor elected by the assembly was also paid by it.[2]

The control of appropriations was not secured by the assembly without frequent disputes.　Much pressure was brought to bear by the governors and the English officials to influence appropriations to suit their own purposes, but the assembly by refusing the appropriations maintained such control as to keep the governors in continual worry to find ways of raising enough money.　It must be said, however, that the governors differed much in their ability to secure money from the assembly.　Chalmers says that in 1715 the standing revenue of £4000 was too small to pay the civil list and that £300 of the king's quit rents were used to help out.[3]

There seems to be no doubt that the assembly knew its power and used it to the advantage of the colonies.　For example when Lord Loudoun, the English general in America, put an embargo on shipping from America to Europe in 1756, the Virginians had 50,000 bushels of wheat on shipboard ready for exportation and it was certain to spoil if the ships did not sail.　Governor Dinwiddie wrote to Loudoun and insisted that the embargo be withdrawn, so far at least as Virginia ships were concerned, for he could get no war supplies from his assembly until the embargo was

[1] Hening, *op. cit.*, i, 280–2.　　　　[2] *Ibid.*, 423, 498, etc.

[3] Chalmers, *Hist. of Rev.*, ii, 71.

removed.   It was argued that if the people lost their grain, they could not pay taxes and the assembly would not vote them.   It seems that the English government supported Dinwiddie in this demand on Loudoun.[1]

In spite of the fact that the legislature used its power over appropriations to force the hands of the governors, it was on the whole tolerably liberal, especially in the matter of military appropriations.   Not only colonial troops for campaigns against the Spanish, French, and Indians, but even the king's troops were supported by appropriations made by the assembly.[2]   The English parliaments of 1757 and 1758 made grants of over £50,000 to repay Virginia for money expended in the war with France,[3] and this did not equal the amount Virginia had spent.   Nevertheless Governor Dinwiddie was much piqued at the way in which the appropriations were made or because they were not larger.   In 1754, writing of the burgesses, he said, " The People here are too much on a republican Spirit.   The House of Burgesses making resolves in disposing of the King's money without the Concurrence of the other Branches of the Legislature, is without Precedent."   He promised to be on guard to prevent any sum being paid except according to his instructions.[4]   He also said an American assembly could not be depended upon to carry out an expedition against the French, because it would not furnish supplies readily and abundantly enough.[5]   On one occasion the burgesses attached to a bill appropriating money a

---

[1] *Dinwiddie, Pap.*, ii, 618, 664–5.

[2] Hening, ii, 471.   Chalmers, (*Pol. Ann.*, 339), says, the assembly of April, 1679, made representations to the king that, inasmuch as they had been compelled to support the soldiers sent over to help Berkeley, and had other great expenses, they were unable to pay the arrears of the quit rents.

[3] Hening, *op. cit.*, vii, 372–3.

[4] *Dinwiddie, Papers*, i, 236.   [5] *Ibid.*, i, 300, 304.

" rider " in the form of a demand that the governor should surrender his fees for granting land patents. The governor declared the rider unconstitutional, though similar methods had been used by the English House of Commons long before.[1]

There is little doubt that the English government, both through instructions to the governors and through vetoes at home, sought to limit the power of the Virginia assembly over revenues and expenditures. The attitude of the assembly on money, as well as on other questions, adopted at a very early period, was that of complete control, even to the point of making colonial law have precedence over certain forms of English law. This is illustrated in the oath prescribed by the assembly of 1631-2 to be given to the commissioners of monthly courts. They were to swear to do justice according to " the lawes and customs of this colony, and as near as may be after the lawes of the realme of England and the statutes thereof made." [2] This would seem to give a loophole for evading the laws of England on the ground that they did not apply to conditions existing in the colonies, and no such evasion of the colony laws was provided for. Again it was enacted in 1643, that no act of court or any proclamation was to be obeyed if it was contrary to any act of the assembly.[3] It is not true that the colonists during a large part of the colonial period were desiring and plotting independence, but it was the natural desire to control their own property and their own affairs, because they believed they knew the conditions better than the royal officials and the home government could; and that led the Virginians to assume control

---

[1] Gardiner, *Student's Hist. of Eng.*, 670. The principle was in use before 1700.

[2] Hening, *op. cit.*, i, 169.

[3] Hening, *op. cit.*, i, 264.

of taxes and appropriations, and to try to dominate the government of the colony. In later years some of the leaders came to believe that the interests of the colony and those of the mother country were not the same and in some respects in direct conflict with each other. Then it was that the thought of independence first came to them.

Appointment and administration, as exercised by the assembly, will be discussed, though briefly, because they show the general tendency of the assembly to take all authority which was not expressly denied to it, and sometimes even to trench on what was denied. In fact the power to do anything outside the regular routine was sure to be claimed by the assembly. There are more examples of this in the very early history of the assembly than later. As the instructions to the governors became more definite on appointments, the power to make them went more fully to the executive.

Instructions to Governor Berkeley (1641) gave him authority to appoint all officers except councilors, captains of forts, the muster-master, and the surveyor-general, most of whom were to be appointed by the king. It is doubtful, however, whether Berkeley used this power to the full extent without consulting the wishes of the assembly.[1]

During the Commonwealth the assembly appointed all of the officers of the colony,[2] though it permitted the parliamentary commissioners to appoint the governor and sec-

---

[1] Sainsbury, *Calendar of State Pap.*, i, 321.

[2] Hening, *op. cit.*, i, 369, note; Ripley, *op. cit.*, 205; Howe, *op. cit.*, 65. Beverley, *op. cit.*, (bk. i, 55,) says, " Notwithstanding this act of Navigation, the Protector never thought the Plantation enough secured; but frequently changed their governors, to prevent their intriguing with the people. So that during the small time of his Protectorship, they had no less than three Governors there, viz., Diggs, Bennett and Matthews." This is wrong. Cromwell appointed none of them. All, unless the first, were elected by the assembly.

retary immediately after the surrender.[1]   After conferring with Colonel Matthews, the Irish and Scotch commissioners of parliament, on November 26, 1653, reported him to the council of state in England as a fit person to be governor of Virginia.   Since this was more than two years before Matthews was appointed governor (Feb., 1656) it seems to indicate that he was practically nominated to the position by the English government long before the assembly elected him.[2]   It may be that all governors during the Commonwealth period were so nominated.   The fact remains however, that the assembly claimed and exercised the power to elect.

In 1655 the assembly, claiming that there was no other authority to do so, granted a pardon.   Tobacco inspectors and county commissioners were now appointed by the assembly instead of by the governor,[3] and John Bond, because of factious and schismatic demeanor, was dismissed from his office of magistrate and made incapable of holding any public trust or employment.[4]   As early as 1643 the legislature claimed the right to remove ministers from their churches.   An act of 1631-2 ordered that captains of arriving ships should be given directions by the executive council, not in its own name, but in the name of the English privy council and of the assembly.

During the last century of the colonial period it was the rule for the burgesses to appoint the treasurer.   In one instance, in 1738, the governor was authorized (in case of a vacancy) to appoint a temporary treasurer.   The person

---

[1] Doyle, *op. cit.*, i, 223.

[2] Edward D. Neill, as cited in *William and Mary Quarterly*, i, 79. Neill does not state his authority.   Robertson and Chalmers seem to hold the idea that the English government controlled the elections.

[3] Hening, *op. cit.*, ii, 132.   [4] *Ibid.*, 39.

so appointed should hold office until the close of the next session.[1]   Such an appointment occurred in 1766, and the temporary treasurer appointed by the governor was afterwards appointed permanently by the assembly.[2]   The fact that the treasurer was appointed by the burgesses and was for a long time also their speaker gave them much control over him.   They even went so far as to claim that no money should be paid out by him except on their order.   This authority was denied them.[3]   In 1677 the king temporarily forbade the treasurer to pay money save on order from himself.   Before Bacon's rebellion the agents of the colony had tried to get a new charter, and the assembly had provided funds with which to pay these agents.   The money was to be paid out on the order of the assembly only, and much of it had already been paid when at a court at Whitehall, July 13, 1677, the king issued orders to the treasurer of Virginia forbidding him to pay this public money without an order from the king in council. It declared that the assembly had not been legally elected. This order was revoked, June 21, 1678.[4]

In 1693 the assembly also appointed the seventeen persons who, with Governor Nicholson, composed the board of trustees of William and Mary College.

The judicial functions of the assembly were more extensive in the early colonial times than later.   The change came in 1683 with the act of the king depriving the assembly of the right to hear appeals from the general court. Before 1683 the assembly showed a strong tendency to subordinate all the courts to itself, even the general court being no exception.   In fact the house of burgesses attempted

---

[1] Hening, *op. cit.*, v, 65.   [2] *Ibid.*, viii, 211.

[3] Hartwell, Bl. & Chil., *op. cit.*, 62.

[4] *McDon. Papers*, v, 122, 237–8.

[5] Fiske, *Old Virginia and Her Neighbors*, ii, 117.

to make itself the supreme court of the colony.   The act of
1643 declaring that acts of courts or proclamations contrary
to acts of the assembly were not to be obeyed, has already
been mentioned.[1]   At the session of 1658 the sheriff of
James City county was ordered not to obey any warrant
unless signed by the speaker of the house; thus the burgesses took charge of the arrests at the capital.[2]   Four
years later it was provided that the first day of each assembly should be given to hearing reports of grand juries,
to inquiring into remissness of juries and courts and into
the manner of executing the laws.[3]   A law of 1641, re-
enacted two years later, provided that no Catholic should
hold office; in case one should secure office, and should refuse to take the oaths of allegiance and supremacy the assembly could try him and upon conviction dismiss him from
office, and besides impose a heavy fine upon him.   This
seems to have been an early form of impeachment.[4]

Laws of 1643 and 1645 provided for appeals to be taken
from the monthly to the quarter courts, and from those to
the assembly.   In case of appeal to the assembly, the appellant must give security that he would appear on the
day set, abide by the judgment, and if he should lose, pay
treble the damages.[5]   By a law of 1647 this was changed
so that appeals might lie to the assembly only in cases involving new points of law, and where the justice of the decision was questioned by the assembly.   All other decis-
ions were to be final in the quarter court.[6]   In 1659 all restrictions were removed, so that appeals for any amount and
for any reason, might go to the assembly.   However, the
appellant, if he lost, must pay not only the costs, but one

---

[1] See p. 165. Hening, *op. cit.*, i, 264.   [2] *Ibid.*, i, 503.
[3] *Ibid.*, ii, 108.   [4] *Ibid.*, i, 268–9.
[5] *Ibid.*, i, 272, 304.   [6] *Ibid.*, 345; ii, 512.

half the value of the debt in addition, as damages to the appellee.[1] This provision was renewed in 1661-2.[2] A decision of the Surrey county court, said to be *ex post facto* in its nature, was reversed in 1659.[3] About the same time the governor and council were made a court of admiralty for all admiralty cases coming within the jurisdiction of the colonial officials.

In some form appeals to the assembly were allowed until May, 1683,[4] when the authority to hear them was taken away by the king. The circumstances that led to this action by the king are as follows. In order to enforce his claim to the Northern Neck of Virginia, Governor Culpeper found it necessary in 1683 to remove the judicial power from the assembly. He fomented a dispute on the judicial power between the council and the house of burgesses, the burgesses saying that the councilors, having passed on cases as members of the general court, could not sit when the case was appealed to the assembly. On the pretext of settling it, the matter was referred to Charles II, who immediately deprived the assembly of all appellate jurisdiction,[5] but provided that in cases involving £100 or over appeal might lie to the king. In spite of this action the burgesses did not immediately give up their claim to hear such cases. In April, 1683, they asked the governor to add councilors to the committee on public claims. The governor summoned the house and said that " he was sorry to see such obstructions at the beginning of the assembly, as were shown by the request for councilors to be added to the committees " of private causes, as the king had ordered no appeal to be

---

[1] Hening, i, 541. This did not apply to Northumberland county because of its remoteness. No case under 3000 pounds of tobacco in value could be appealed from that county.

[2] *Ibid.*, ii, 65–6.

[3] *Ibid.*, i, 516.

[4] *Ibid.*, iii, 550.

[5] *Ibid.*, iii, 550–1.

allowed from the general court to the assembly. The burgesses said that they knew of no such orders of the king
and asked to see the instructions. Meantime, in order that
the house might be united, it ordered that no member was
to leave James City without permission from the speaker.[1]
Nevertheless, the appeals from the general court to the assembly ceased, and the house lost the place of supreme court.
However, the committee on claims became a permanent factor in the house and through the courts of claims in the
counties and petitions therefrom, a vast amount of business
that was partly judicial in character was done.

The question of appeals to England still continued to be
a source of trouble. In 1704 the governor objected to an
act of a previous assembly as an invasion of the prerogative, in that it prevented the king from establishing courts
of record other than those recognized by that legislature,
and did not recognize appeals to the crown. The governor
asked that changes be made to meet these objections.[2] In
1707 the board of trade said that the act would not pass.[3]

In a certain sense cases of contempt of the house were
treated as judicial matters, therefore they will be considered in connection with that topic. Persons outside of the
house were often declared guilty of contempt of the house
and punished therefor. A few examples will illustrate.
It seems that some persons had said that the acts of assembly had no binding force and therefore that no one was
obliged to obey them. An act of 1682 imposed heavy penalties on any one who was convicted of such offense.[4] In
1744 John Austin of King William county threatened to

---

[1] *Va. Mag. of Hist.*, x, 238. See also Hartwell, Bl. & Chil., *op.
cit.*, 25.

[2] *Jour. of Coun. as Upper House*, i (Apr., 1704?), 14.

[3] Chalmers, *Hist. of Rev.*, i, 318.   [4] Hening, ii, 501–2.

raise a body of men and to drive the burgesses into Hampton river. For this he was brought before the house, acknowledged his folly and having made his submission he paid the fees and was released.[1] During the session of 1772 a witness before the committee on religion was arrested, notwithstanding such witnesses were supposed to be exempt from arrest. Roger Gregory who caused the arrest and the under sheriff who made the arrest were declared guilty of high contempt and of breach of the privilege of the house. The under sheriff was later excused and upon Gregory's declaration that he did not know of the rule, he was excused on paying fees.[2] Some of the many cases of breach of privilege and the punishment therefor have been referred to above.[3]

Enough has been said to show that the judicial power of the assembly was quite extensive before 1683; that at that date the king deprived the assembly of the right to hear appeals; that, in spite of the loss of that power, the burgesses, through the committee of claims and courts of claim, continued to exercise considerable judicial power. When, in 1775, the royal authority was overthrown, the assembly, as in 1652, assumed the entire control of the government, the judicial power included.

Treaty-making in the strict sense can exist between two or more independent nations only. It would therefore not be a power possessed by the colonies. Yet something in the nature of a treaty, perhaps better called an agreement, was resorted to quite frequently in the colonies. Since the legislature took part in some of these, brief reference to them will be made.

At the session of 1643, agreements regulating commerce,

[1] *Jour. of Burg.*, Sep., 1744, 38, 44.

[2] *Ibid.*, 1772, 54, 57–8.   [3] See pp. 89–91, 142–143.

made with Maryland two years previous, were ratified.[1]
Three years later a treaty was made with the Indians and
penalties were provided for its violation.[2]   The arrangements with the parliamentary commissions at the surrender
of 1652 were in a certain sense treaties.[3]   In 1666 the governor and council made agreements with Maryland and
Carolina on the cessation of tobacco planting, apparently
with the consent of the assembly.[4]   It is quite possible that
most of these arrangements were made by the executive and
ratified by the assembly.   In the eighteenth century, the
royal power having become more firmly fixed, and a governor or deputy being nearly always present, this became
the rule.   Such agreements or treaties as were found necessary were made by the executive, the assembly having no
part except helping to carry them into effect, or possibly refusing to do so.   Several treaties with the Indians were
made during this time.

The establishment of two houses occurred about 1680.
Before that time burgesses, councilors and governor, all sat
together in one house.   Nevertheless, before 1680 there are
a few references in the records which indicate different
groups, though probably not a separation into two houses.

The assembly of November, 1647, speaks of " all members of both houses," but it is known that the two groups
did not sit separately when legislating.[5]   Lodge says, " The
burgesses granted two houses to Berkeley " in 1643,[6] but
Doyle thinks they voted together as before.[7]   When the
burgesses assumed all the power in 1652, it was voted that
the governor and council should be members of that as-

---

[1] Hening, *op. cit.*, i, 276.   [2] *Ibid.*, i, 323–6.

[3] See articles, *ibid.*, i, 363–8.   [4] *Ibid.*, ii, 250–3.

[5] *Ibid.*, i, 341.

[6] Lodge, *Eng. Col. in Amer.*, 15.   [7] Doyle, *op. cit.*, i, 218.

sembly, but that they must take the oath the burgesses took.[1] It will be remembered that when, in 1659, a committee which had been appointed to revise the laws was about to report, the question arose as to whether the laws should first be considered by the burgesses in private instead of in the presence of the governor and council with the result that the governor and council were excluded.[2] These things, along with the separate control of the burgesses over revenue and expenditure, indicate a growing independence of the two branches, with separate sittings for certain matters, but with no complete separation before 1680.

Beverley[3] says that the separation came with the dispute over the right of the burgesses to hear appeals from the courts. It seems that the burgesses thought the council, having passed on the cases as a court, ought not to be present in the assembly when the burgesses heard them. This led to a separation for other purposes as well, and the two houses became firmly established.

I*T* will be recalled that the first method of legislating for Virginia, that by the company and by councils did not recognize the colonists as self-governing; but when the step which did give such recognition was taken in 1619, that step created a precedent which the Stuart kings were bound to recognize. Because the colonists were represented in the legislature, and later largely dominated that body, and because the legislature became more and more important in the directing of all colonial matters, the colonists soon became important factors in the government of Virginia, and such they continued to be during the remainder of the

[1] Hening, *op. cit.*, i, 373; Howe, *op. cit.*, 65; Campbell, C., *op. cit.*, 238.

[2] Hening, *op. cit.*, i, 497; Howe, *op. cit.*, 66; Howison, *op. cit.*, 310; Campbell, C., *op. cit.*, 238.   [3] Beverley, 82; Doyle, i, 262-3.

colonial period. The Virginia colony was a good illustration of the vigorous assertion of the Anglo-Saxon spirit of self-rule and adaptation to environment. The long conflict between government by appointees of a distant power, and government by representatives chosen by the people themselves, ending as it did in victory for the people, shows that among English people in Virginia at least the principle of representative government was stronger than absolutism.

At first, as the legislature sat in one house, with governor, councilors and burgesses all together, the people's representatives did not stand out distinctly from the other parts of the body; but after about sixty years the legislature separated into two houses, those members who were chosen by the people as usual becoming the lower house or the house of burgesses. This separation gave more opportunity for successful contests by the elective branch against the appointive branch of the legislature and against the other parts of the government. The efforts of the burgesses to gain power for themselves and for the people now became more noticeable. These efforts culminated in the revolution of 1776 when the legislature was the center of opposition to the acts of the English government and ultimately seized all the functions of government and reorganized it on a new basis; a basis of complete independence and complete control by the people. Thus ended the long struggle for power which the people through their representatives had carried on.

While these struggles were going on, the internal organization of the legislature itself, the details of electing its members, their qualifications, their privileges and restrictions, the details of organization and procedure, the place of the governor and council, the all-important subject of the control of public moneys, were being worked out and settled. When the revolution came the Virginia legislature had developed all the essential features of a law making body.

Thus it will be seen that in the preceding discussion an attempt has been made to give an historical account of the origin of the legislature of colonial Virginia, and of its internal development from the beginning of government in Virginia to the revolution of 1776.

BIBLIOGRAPHY.

NOTE.—All the books in the following list have been used, but those marked with a star are referred to in the footnotes. It will be evident that the study is based chiefly on Hening's *Statutes*, and the various journals of the two houses.

*Archiologia Americana, Series IV, History of the English Colonies in America, edited by St. Clair Clarke and Peter Force, 6 vols., Washington, D. C., 1837.

*Ancient Virginia Records (MSS.) in Lib. of Congress. Typewritten copy Va. Hist. Soc. Lib.

Andrews, E. Benjamin, History of the United States, 2 vols., New York, 1894.

*Ballagh, James Curtis, White Servitude in the Colony of Virginia, Johns Hopkins University Studies XIII, Series No. VI-VII, Baltimore, 1895.

*Bancroft, George, History of the United States, 6 vols., New York, 1888.

Bancroft Transcripts, Virginia Official Correspondence, 2 vols., 1752-1773, 1768-1776. [Very largely letters of governor to home office, and much of it concerns executive and administrative business, but occasionally refers to assembly or acts thereof. Many letters to Lords of Trade; others to various Secretaries of State.] MSS. Lib. of Cong.

*Beverley, Robert, The History and Present State of Virginia, London, 1705.

*Bishop, Cortlandt F., Colonial Elections, Columbia College Series, New York, 1903.

Bourne, E. G., Demarkation Line of Alexander VI, in Yale Review, May, 1892. Same in Essays in Historical Criticism.

Bozman, John Leeds, The History of Maryland, 2 vols., Baltimore, 1837.

*Brown, Alexander, Genesis of the United States, 2 vols., Boston and New York, 1891.

*Brown, Alexander, The First Republic in America. Houghton, Mifflin & Co., Boston, 1898.

*Brown, Alexander, English Politics in Early Virginia History. Houghton, Mifflin & Co., Boston, 1901.

*Bruce, Philip Alexander, Economic History of Virginia in the Seventeenth Century, 2 vols., New York, 1896.

Bryan, J. S., Address to Va. St. Bar Asso., July, 1898, on "Statutes Prior to this Century" (19th). Richmond, 1898.

Bryant and Gay, Popular History of the United States, 4 vols., London, 1876.

Bryce, James, American Commonwealth, 2 vols., New York, 1895.

Burk, John, The History of Virginia, 4 vols., Petersburg, Va., 1804.

*Campbell, Charles, History of the Colony and Ancient Dominion of Virginia, Philadelphia, 1860.

Campbell, J. W., A History of Virginia from its Discovery to 1781, Philadelphia and Petersburg, Va., 1813.

*Chalmers, Geo., Political Annals of the Present United Colonies from their settlement to the Peace of 1763, Book I, J. Bowen, London, 1780.

*Chalmers, Geo., Political Annals of the Present United Colonies, etc., Book II. Printed in the Collections of the New York Hist. Soc. for 1868. Publication Fund Series, vol. i.

*Chalmers, Geo., An Introduction to the History of the Revolt of the Amer. Colonies, 2 vols., James Munroe & Co. Boston, 1845. (Written but suppressed, 1782.)

*Chalmers, Geo., Opinions of Eminent Lawyers on Various Points of Jurisprudence on Colonies, Fisheries and Commerce of Great Britain. Goodrich & Co., Burlington, 1858.

Chandler, Julian A. C., Representation in Virginia. New York, Baltimore, 1896.

*Channing, Edward, Town and County Government in the English Colonies of North America, J. H. U. S., II Series, IX. Baltimore, 1884.

Colonial Records of Virginia, Richmond, 1874. Also found in collection of New York Historical Society, II Series, vol. iii, Part 1, New York, 1857.

*Cooke, John Esten, Virginia: A History of the People (Am. Commonwealth Series), Boston, 1888.

*De Jarnette, Papers from British Record Office 1606-1691. 2 vols.; I, 1606-1674; II, 1675-1691. Va. and Md. Col. Rec. (Va. St. Lib.).

Denniston, David, Constitution of the Sixteen States in 1800, Newburgh, 1800.

*Dinwiddie Papers, Va. Hist. Col., 2 vols., Richmond, 1883.

*Doyle, J. A., English Colonies in America, 3 vols., New York, 1889.

Drake, Samuel Adams, The Making of Virginia and the Middle Colonies, 1578-1701, New York, 1893.

*Fiske, John, Old Virginia and Her Neighbors, 2 vols., Boston.

*Foote, William Henry, Sketches of Virginia Historical and Biographical, Philadelphia, 1850.

*Force, Peter, Tracts on American History, 4 vols., Washington, D. C., 1844.

*Gardiner, Samuel Rawdon, Student's History of England, London, 1895.

Grahame, James, History of the United States of North America, 4 vols., London, 1836.

Green, J. R., History of the English People, 4 vols., New York, 1878.

*Hamilton, Alexander, The Federalist, New York, 1892.

*Hart, A. B., Practical Essays on American Government, New York, 1894.

*Hartwell, Henry, Blair, James, Chilton, Edward, The Present State of Virginia and the College, London. Printed for John Wyat, at the Rose in St. Paul's Churchyard, 1727.

*Hening, William Waller, Statutes at Large of Virginia, 1619-1792, 13 vols., New York, 1823.

Henry, W. W., The First Legislative Assembly in America, Va. Mag. Hist., ii, 55-67.

Henry, W. W., Life of Patrick Henry, 2 vols.

Higginson, Thomas Wentworth, American Explorers, Boston, 1877.

*Hildredth, Richard, History of the United States of America, 6 vols., New York, 1882.

*Holmes, Abiel, Annals of America, 2 vols., Cambridge, 1825.

Howard, Geo. E., Local Constitutional History of the United States, Baltimore, 1889.

*Howe, Henry, Historical Collections of Virginia, Charleston, S. C., 1845.

*Howison, Robert R., A History of Virginia, 2 vols., Philadelphia, 1846.

*Ingle, Edward, Virginia Local Institutions, J. H. U. S., III Series, II-III, Baltimore, 1885.

Jefferson, Thomas, Notes on the State of Virginia, New York, 1801.

Johnson, Alexander, in New Princeton Review, September, 1887.

Jones, Rev. Hugh, The Present State of Virginia, London, 1724. Reprinted by Jos. Sabin, New York, 1865. [Not much value for government; good for church and social customs.]

*Journals of House of Burgesses: [List of by J. F. Jameson in Report of Am. Hist. Assoc., 1897, 432-437.]

Mar. 1, 1693 (MSS.). *Va. St. Lib.*

May 22, 1740; May 6, 1742; Oct. 27, 1748; Feb. 27, 1752; Nov. 1, 1753; Aug. 22, 1754; Oct. 17, 1754; May 1, 1755; Aug. 5, 1755; Oct. 27, 1755; Mar. 25, 1756; Sept. 20, 1756; Apr. 14, 1757; Mar. 30, 1758; Sept. 14, 1758; Feb. 22, 1759; Nov. 1, 1759. *Lib. of Cong.*

Oct. 6, 1760; Dec. 11, 1760 (one day); Mar. 5, 1761; Jan. 14, 1762; Oct. 30, 1764; May 8, 1769; Nov. 7, 1769; May 21, 1770; Feb. 16, 1772; Mar. 4, 1773; May 5, 1774. *Lib. of Cong.*

Sept. 4, 1744; Feb. 20, 1745-6. *Va. St. Lib.*

Feb. 22, 1752; Nov. 3, 1753; Feb. 16, 1754; Oct. 17, 1754; May 1, 1755; Aug. 5, 1755; Oct. 27, 1755; Mar. 25, 1756; Apr. 14, 1757; Mar. 30, 1758. *Va. St. Lib.*

Nov. 3, 1761; Jan. 14, 1762; Mar. 30, 1762; Nov. 2, 1762; May 19, 1763; Jan. 12, 1764; Oct. 30, 1764; May 1, 1765. *Va. St. Lib.*

Nov. 7, 1769; May 21, 1770; July 11, 1771; Feb. 10, 1772. *Va. St. Lib.*

Mar. 4, 1773; May 5, 1774; June 1, 1775; Oct. 12, 1775; Mar. 7, 1776; May 6, 1776. [Last three just a few members met and, not having a quorum for business, adjourned. These are manuscripts in Va. St. Lib., but a copy made by W. W. Scott, 1902, then State Librarian, and certified by him to the Society of Colonial Dames, was used in taking notes.]

Feb., 1772. *Lenox Library, New York.*

Journal of Proceedings of Convention of Delegates for Counties and Corporations of Colony of Virginia, held at Richmond Town, in the County of Henrico, on the 20th of March, 1775; July 17, 1775; Dec. 1, 1775; May 6, 1776. Reprinted by a resolution of H. of Del., Feb. 24, 1816. Pages 1-4 missing; only 8 pages.

Journal of Proceedings of Convention of Delegates, held at the town of Richmond, in the Colony of Virginia, Friday, the 1st of Dec., 1775, and afterwards, by adjournment, in the city of Williamsburg. Williamsburg, Printed by Alexander Purdie. (No date.) Va. Hist. Soc. (This is included in the volume just before.)

*Journals of Council of Virginia as Upper House. [These are manuscript copies made of incomplete records in the State Library at Richmond, and are in the Library of Va. Hist. Soc. They have been carefully compared with the originals by Mr. W. G. Stanard, Librarian of Va. Hist. Soc., and are correct copies. They are arranged in three volumes, as follows: I, 1685-1720; II, 1722-1747; III, 1748-1767.]

*Keith, Sir William, The History of the British Plantations in America, etc. Part I, History of Virginia, London. Printed by Society for Encouragement of Learning, 1738. [Mostly concerned with period before 1624.]

Lalor, John J., Cyclopedia of Political Science, 3 vols., New York, 1890.

*Laws of Virginia Now in Force, London, 1662. Lenox Lib., N. Y. [Copies in Lenox, Bar Assoc. Phil., Brit. Museum, and one other copy known.]

*Lodge, Henry Cabot, The English Colonies in America, New York, 1891.

Lossing, Benj. J., Pictorial Field Book of the Revolution, 2 vols., New York, 1860.

Lossing, Benj. J., Harper's Popular Cyclopedia of United States History, 2 vols., New York, 1890.

*Ludwell Papers, 6 vols., Va. Hist. Soc. Lib.

*McDonald Papers. From Brit. Rec. Office, 7 vols., MSS. I, Miscell., 1619-1626; II, Miscell., 1627-1640; III and IV vols. missing for many years; V, Virginia, 1675-1681; VI, Virginia, 1681-1685; VII, Virginia, 1683-1695. *Va. St. Lib.*

Marshall, John, Life of George Washington, 5 vols., Philadelphia, 1804.

Minor, W. G. and B. B., in Southern Literary Messenger, VII and X, Richmond, 1835.

*Miscellaneous MSS., marked U-V, in Va. Hist. Soc. gives records of one of committees of burgesses for Feb., 1727. These probably only committee records now preserved 76-77, 80-85, etc.

Moran, Thomas Francis, Rise and Development of the Bicameral System in America, J. H. U. S., XIII, Baltimore, 1895.

Neill, Edward D., History of the Virginia Company of London, Albany, 1869.

*Neill, Edward D., Virginia Carolorum, Albany, 1886.

New York Colonial Records, edited by E. B. O'Callaghan, 14 vols., Albany, 1856-61.

*Osgood, Herbert L., The American Colonies in the Seventeenth Century, 2 vols., N. Y., 1904.

*Palmer, William P., Calendar of Virginia State Papers and Other Manuscripts, 1752-1807, 9 vols., Richmond, 1875-90.

Parton, James, Life of Thomas Jefferson, Boston, 1889.

Pitkin, Timothy, Political and Civil History of the United States of America, 2 vols., New Haven, 1825.

*Poore, Benj. Perley, Charters and Constitutions of the United States, 2 vols., Washington, 1877.

Preston, Howard W., Documents Illustrative of American History, 1606-1863, New York, 1893.

*Randolph Papers, 3 vols.; [I and II are copies of records of Lon. Co. from 1619 on; III is miscellaneous charters, instructions, etc., concerning the early period.] *Va. Hist. Soc. Lib.*

*Records of the London Company, MSS., 2 vols. Lib. of Cong.

*Ripley, William Zebina, The Financial History of Virginia, 1606-1776, Columbia College Studies, New York, 1893.

*Robertson, William, History of America, 2 vols., Albany, 1822.

*Robinson MSS., *Va. Hist. Soc. Lib.*

*Rymer, Thom., and Sanderson, Robert, Foedera, Conventions, Literae, et Cujuscunque Genesis Acta Publica inter Reges Angliae et alios quosvis, Imperatores, Reges, Pontifices, etc.
2d Edit., 20 vols. (last 4), Lond., 1727-35.

*Sainsbury, W. Noel, Calendar of State Papers, Colonial Series, 1574-1696, 9 vols. [Relate to Am. and W. India.] Longmans, Green, Longman & Roberts, Lon., 1860-1903.

Sainsbury Papers [11 vols. unnumbered and 8 partly numbered. Longer abstracts than appear in printed vols., and covering time from 1573-1730.] *MSS. Va. St. Lib.*

Scott, Eben G., The Development of Constitutional Liberty in the English Colonies of America, New York, 1890.

*Seeley, J. R., Expansion of England, London, 1891.

Smith, John, General History of Virginia, New England, and the Summer Isles, 1624, reprinted by Edward Arber, English Scholars Library, Birmingham, 1884.

*Spotswood, Alexander, Official Letters of, 2 vols., Va. Hist. Soc. Collect., Richmond, Va., 1882.

*Stanard, Wm. G., and Mary Newton, The Colonial Virginia Register, List of Governors, Councilors and Other Higher Officials, and Members of House of Burg. Joel Munsell's Sons, Albany, N. Y., 1902.

*Stith, William, History of the First Discovery and Settlement of Virginia, Williamsburg, 1747.

*Stokes, Anthony, A View of the Constitution of the British Colonies in N. Amer. and W. Indies. B. White, London, 1783.

*Story, Joseph, Commentaries on the Constitution of the United States, 2 vols., Boston, 1891.

Thwaites, Reuben G., The Colonies, New York, 1895.

Trumbull, J. Hammond, The True-Blue Laws of Connecticut and New Haven, Hartford, 1876.

*Tyler, L. G., England in America, N. Y., 1905.

Tyler, M. C., Patrick Henry (American Statesman Series), New York, 1890.

*Virginia Historical Collections, New Series, 7 vols., Richmond.

*Virginia Magazine of History and Biography, 12 vols., Richmond.

Weeks, Stephen B., Southern Quakers and Slavery, J. H. U. S., extra volume XIV, Baltimore, 1893.

Winder, F. A., Virginia Manuscripts from British Record Office, 1607-1776. 2 vols., Va. St. Lib. Vol. I, 1607-1676; Vol. II, Bacon's Rebellion.

Winsor, Justin, Narrative and Critical History of America, 8 vols., especially volume III, New York, 1884.

Wirt, Wm., Sketches of the Life and Character of Patrick Henry. Phila., 1817, James Webster, Pub.